CONCILIUM
Religion in the Seventies

CONCILIUM

Religion in the Seventies

EDITORIAL DIRECTORS: Edward Schillebeeckx (Dogma) •
Herman Schmidt (Liturgy) • Alois Müller (Pastoral) •
Hans Küng (Ecumenism) • Franz Böckle (Moral Theology) •
Johannes B. Metz (Church and World) • Roger Aubert (Church
History) • Teodoro Jimenez Urresti (Canon Law) • Christian
Duquoc (Spirituality) • Pierre Benoît and Roland Murphy
(Scripture)

CONSULTING EDITORS: Marie-Dominique Chenu • ✠Carlo
Colombo • Yves Congar • Andrew Greeley • Jorge Mejía •
Karl Rahner • Roberto Tucci

EXECUTIVE SECRETARY: (Awaiting new appointment),
Arksteestraat 3–5, Nijmegen, The Netherlands

Volume 66: Church and World

EDITORIAL BOARD: Johannes Baptist Metz • Willi Oelmüller •
Werner Bröker • Jos Arntz • Alfonso Alvarez Bolado • Paul
Blanquart • Henri Bouillard • Daniel Callahan • Bertrand de
Clercq • Joseph Comblin • Etienne Cornélis • Adolf Darlap •
Heimo Dolch • Albert Dondeyne • Dominique Dubarle •
Iring Fetscher • Heinrich Fries • Giulio Girardi • Jean-Yves Jolif •
Andreas van Melsen • Charles Moeller • Christopher Mooney •
Maurice Nédoncelle • Francis O'Farrell • Raymond Panikkar •
Norbert Schiffers • Heinz Schlette • Alexander Schwan • Juan
Segundo • Robert Spaemann • David Tracy • Josef Trütsch •
Roberto Tucci • Jan Walgrave • Bernhard Welte

PERSPECTIVES OF A
POLITICAL ECCLESIOLOGY

Edited by
Johannes B. Metz

Herder and Herder

1971
HERDER AND HERDER NEW YORK
232 Madison Avenue, New York 10016

CONTENTS

PART III

DOCUMENTATION CONCILIUM

Editorial

1. Is what Guardini called the "Church's century" turning into the "lapsers' century"? Recent theological debate has given the concept of "Church" a great deal of attention; perhaps too much? There is probably no other theme so emotively overloaded. And yet while all this frantic discussion is going on among the theologians, thousands are defecting from the Church. Increasingly, people are becoming reluctant to identify themselves with the Church, or with whatever it is they understand by the term. The number of Christians who believe themselves to constitute the Church, and act accordingly, grows ever smaller, and this in spite of such slogans as "the common priesthood of believers", the Church as "the people of God", and in spite of all the emphasis on the importance of the laity in the Church. Vatican II, it seems, has already slipped into history, and not just for those who anyway would have preferred it never to have happened, but also for the widely differing range of reform groups and movements within the Church itself.

2. In such a situation, what is the ecclesiologist to do? How is he to avoid being traduced into a wholly false relationship to the object of his study, namely the Church? The arguments are so many and varied that there is great danger of eclecticism, if not sectarianism. Or is the end product of ecclesiology always only itself and its own interests: something nice for professors of theology, as though the Church existed for them alone, or as though the New Testament were written for exegetes alone?

Might it be thought possible to save the situation I have so

7

briefly outlined by looking at it meditatively from the standpoint
of the Bible? A number of people have tried it in the expectation
of finding there some form of guidance as to how we might
understand the contemporary Church. Neither can it be denied
that constant reference to the biblical witness is essential, and that
even for the present position of the Church recourse to the Bible
can release useful and liberating insights. However, we have to
beware of corner cutting; the theologian is not entitled to ignore
the enormous difference between the Church we have today and
the unique and unrepeatable situation that obtained in the biblical
era. That is to say that we may not presume to be able to determine
the content and object of the biblical testimony in connection with
the Church without reference to anything outside that testimony,
or that we may then apply the insights gained to the present situation so as to be able to question the shortcomings that then appear
to be revealed. We must not forget that the very differences between our situation and those that obtained in biblical times are
the impulses that require us once again to examine what the Bible
has to say about the Church.

There are also those whose concern for reform is unaccom-
panied by any interest in the application of theological discipline
to the process of determining its nature. However understandable
impatience with theology may be, the dangers of careless enthusiasm seem to me to be very obvious: ecclesiology is at once reduced
to little more than the tactical expression of how the present
situation might be changed. "New practices" have to be accompanied by new forms of commemoration, a new actualization of
the historical circumstances in which the Church exists. Otherwise the new practices themselves merely come and go, become
symbols only of some new ecclesial reality without having created
the reality itself, and ultimately of course they can be absorbed
or rejected by whatever system is dominant without having
changed the system in any effective way. In this respect, it seems
quite possible that the promoters of Church reform could learn
something from the negative experiences of protest movements
in the social field.

There are others, again, who pursue ecclesiological studies only
as a means of bringing criticism to bear on the Church and on
official Church theology. The Church does of course have to ask

itself to what extent it is able or prepared to allow freedom to its critics and to allow its members to behave like the adults they are. I am convinced for my own part that theology rightly exercises a critical function with regard to ecclesiastical realities: thus, for example, theology must insist that the now favoured imputation to the Church of political neutrality and political innocence is either dangerously misleading or is a conscious attempt to disguise existing political Church alliances. Similarly, theology should resist the attempt to determine ecclesiastical thought and life forms through the products of cognitive and operative alien systems. Such an attempt could very well lead to the end of ecclesiology.

In extreme contrast with the situation I have been describing with regard to the present situation of the Church is a type of heightened ecclesiological fundamentalism and positivism: a theology of the Church that sees its role as that of legitimizing and defending the dominant Roman version of how things ought to be. To these people, the Church's present crisis is regarded as a reason for persevering through thick and thin, not as an impulse to conversion and renewal. The result is to range against what might be an exaggerated drive towards adaptation a similarly exaggerated orthodoxy coupled with emotional demands for loyalty. The ecclesiological image of "the Church of sinners", which is a constant appeal for renewal addressed to head and members, is in this way secretly transposed into a vision of the select community of the saints. Ecclesiologcial fundamentalism of this type is suspect because it induces blindness in respect of the real causes of stagnation and defection and because it hinders painful but necessary changes. Thus it can be seen that in the end this attitude is no more loyal to the Roman Church than that of a theology critical of the Church. It betrays or renders ineffective the freedom of theology within the Church—a freedom that is not simply freedom from the Church, or freedom to speak against the Church. The freedom that theology needs in the Church is rather that of anticipation, of warning; such freedom liberates theology not from the true interests of the Church's mission and its message, but enables it to anticipate in a hypothetical but creative way situations that will befall the Church.

3. The object of this issue of *Concilium* is to present an account of "Aspects of a Fundamental-theological Ecclesiology". It

develops "Aspects of a Theological Interpretation of the Present Situation of the Church". We have not tried to be exhaustive, and this not just because the theme is more or less inexhaustive, but also because some of the contributions we had hoped to have were not ready in time. Our overall objective is to show that from the viewpoint of fundamental theology, ecclesiology has changed radically (as compared with the classical apologetical treatises on the Church).

A fundamental theology that includes within its sphere of reference and discussion all the problems and questions of the contemporary Church will not treat the Church as a monolithic entity. It will speak less exclusively than before about "the" Church. And in saying that I am thinking not so much of the plurality of Christian Churches generally, but rather of the necessary differentiations within our Church alone—with regard, therefore, to the different forms the Church can take in the whole sphere of Church life, and with regard, therefore, to the most varied Church communities, groups, movements, and so on. It appears that nowadays it is in these spontaneous groups that the Church is best able to show mobility and a readiness to learn, and to develop an understanding of non-Church religiosity. Much of the impulse towards new life and renewal comes to us from these groups. But at the same time, firm connections between such groups and the Church as a whole can prevent the groups from becoming mere sub-cultures within an increasingly churchless society, a situation in which they could easily lose their Christian image. How will the Church survive its own minority situation? In my view, much hangs on the answer to this question. And in this connection it seems to me important to see whether the Church succeeds in absorbing within itself the inspirational power of religious minorities both of the present and from history. It is possible, for instance, that the so-called sect and heretic hunts of former days have been undervalued by a one-sided ecclesiocentricity. Could they not be made use of in some new form? Perhaps by looking at their history we would learn that to become a minority is also to be given a new chance.[1]

[1] The extent to which the larger Churches are increasingly in danger of becoming sects in a theologically negative sense is a question I tried to explain in my contribution to *Kirche in Prozess der Aufklärung* (1970).

A fundamental theology that is true to the way in which the Church has presented iself to the world in history and in fact must take account of the criticism that was initiated through awareness of this same Church history. In many contemporary theories of society the Church is presented as an organization of historically mixed notions and understandings of itself, as institutionalized tabooing of knowledge and productive inquiry; it is seen as an anti-emancipatory leftover with a merely simulated interest in freedom and the "upright stance" of man, as a narcotic in a suffering and unjust world.

Further, such theories refer to the growing lack of function demonstrated by the Church. The dominant image becomes one of indifference and of well-meaning politeness, a caricature of the sympathy offered to the dying. Even militant communists are now reluctant to fight against such an apparently meaningless organization, while in futurological discussions the Church is hardly considered at all. And even liberal Christians preach irrevocable "defection from the Church", and recommend an eclectic cult Christianity as a remedy against the pressures of our Western way of life. How much sense is there in all this? Are such notions merely thrown up by the pressures of the times or do the judgments they embody show evidence of the permanent state of siege of the Church in the world, the always agonized situation of the Church of the crucified Lord of which every believer must most seriously take account?

In my opinion, we should not be too quick to present this theological answer for it easily overlooks the deep-reaching roots of the dominant attitude towards the Church: the historical experience of the Church, the memory of the disappointments to which it has given rise, the historical conscience of generations, a conscience that reminds us of the suspect alliances the Church has entered into with the major political powers and of the ambiguous impression of the Church: not so much a religion to believe in, more a self-compensating religion.

The factors need to be borne constantly in mind for, whatever we might think, they represent memories that will not be stilled. It is they, not historical evidence of the founding of the Church and of the apostolic succession, that represent the primary historical-hermeneutical problem for a contemporary ecclesiology. And the problem will not be solved via a "better" or "more subtle" interpretation of the Church's past, but only through the "proof of the spirit and power" of a new praxis, through painful change. It is here that the true spirit of Church reform is rooted. It is not concerned with cheaply-bought notions of modernity and relevance but with the question of the historical identity and continuity of the Church and its believed mission. And by Church here we mean first and foremost we ourselves, we Christians, who seek to live in memory of Jesus Christ and for whom the notion of a wholly institutionless and churchless handing on of this memory (which would make the individual the exclusive bearer of the message) appears illusionary.[2]

JOHANNES BAPTIST METZ

[2] I have taken this last paragraph word for word from the text of my address during the Concilium Congress in Brussels, 1970.

Translated by Mark Hollebone

PART I
ARTICLES

François Houtart

Extra-Ecclesial Interests and Maintaining the *Status Quo* of the Churches

THE Churches are institutions and they are inserted in a cultural and social context. Now any institution is a social construction, which means that it cannot be understood, explained or even defined without reference to the universe in which it was born or in which it develops. No institution is a self-contained entity, even though each is tempted to consider itself as such. There is, moreover, a constant interaction, conscious or otherwise, between the various institutions, and the global culture of the human group is the result of this. These considerations, when applied to the Church, do not place in question the other dimensions of its reality, in particular its divine origin.

Although one can go along with Peter Berger[1] when he says that the Churches find in society viability structures, i.e., a social and cultural basis of their existence, it must also be affirmed that the social, economic and political systems also need structures of viability situated in the ethical sphere. Gandhi affirmed this when he said that attacking the moral bases of a political system was very effective. This is the role ideology plays in offering to the group a reading of its past as of its future and it is not surprising that in the Western societies the Churches are associated with this function.

To take concrete examples: the presence of President Nixon at one of Billy's Graham's mass meetings shortly after the intervention in Cambodia, as also his visit to Pope Paul VI shortly

[1] Peter Berger, *The Social Reality of Religion* (London, 1969), p. 41.

before the elections in November 1970, are situated in this perspective. President Caetano's explanations concerning the visit
by the leaders of the liberation movements of the Portuguese
colonies to Paul VI, and the opposition of the Belgian bourgeoisie to Cardinal Suenens because the latter in their eyes was
straining the principle of authority, are also clear expressions of
this.

There is then mutual influence. The established regimes
bring a certain amount of weight to bear on ecclesial institutions
which might tend to oppose social change. Some transformations
in the Churches themselves may appear to be social menaces. A
very subtle wealth of mutual interests comes into play and the
Churches secretly uphold values different from those they proclaim. In the case of rapid change, the social system on which,
at least to a considerable degree, the Churches themselves are
modelled, is placed in question and the risk arises of solidarity
between the groups or classes in favour of the *status quo* and the
ecclesiastical organization.

This is a constant dilemma found throughout history, even
where the Christian Churches are numerically in the minority,
but where they were born at the same time as colonial enterprise.
Without doubt a distinction must be made in the Churches as
institutions between the many levels and different strata, but
this is true of any institution. Profound internal differences exist,
especially in a period which makes a plurality of objectives possible. It is then indispensable if we wish to embark on an attempt
at explanation of the liaisons and to go beyond mere description,
to employ an historical perspective and have recourse to a sociology of religion.

I. RELIGION IN SOCIAL CHANGE

In the traditional societies, the symbiosis between nature and
society integrates the latter in the representations of cosmic de-
terminism. This provokes in return the elaboration of a system
of explanation of natural phenomena through the creation of a
mythical universe, reflection and guarantor of the social system.
The worlds of the living, of the dead, of the spirits or of the
divinities intermingle closely and become hierarchically graded

according to a real or mythical power over natural and social phenomena.

The human groups have practically no possibility of formulating and pursuing their own collective objectives. It can be said that social attitude are founded essentially on the observance of norms of which the social system, and in particular authority, assures conformity. The integration between nature, society and mythical universe make sacred the guarantors of the social organization and of its symbolism. Conversely, such an interpretation makes nature a social category.[2]

Thus it will easily be understood that the conquest of man over nature is considered a sacrilege or as having to be accomplished through the mediation of a rite permitting the appropriation of a sacred power. The symbiosis between a natural universe so full of the sacred and the organization of social life is such that all the events of the life of the human communities are also governed by gods or by spirits. In such a system the natural order and the social order are homogeneous and rest on the observance of common behavioural norms.[3] A greater part of the myths of the traditional religions are expressions of this reality and they are found in many different contexts.

This vision of the universe doubtless leaves a certain latitude for changes situated in the very heart of the fundamental perspective. Certainly civilizations, dynasties and political systems are seen to succeed one another, but the element of continuity remains the relation with the sacred, considered, under multiple and changing forms, as inherent to the physical or social world. A "desacralized" perspective, where man acquires an autonomy in the utilization of nature and in the organization of society, signifies then a real rupture.

The Judaeo-Christian tradition, one might think, was well-armed to accept a civilization valuing the responsibility of man. Do not several contemporary theologians say that the real root

[2] E. Durkheim and M. Maus, "De quelques formes primitives de classi-fication", in *Année Sociologique* (1901–02), p. 1.

[3] Cf. the descriptions of Levy-Bruhl, *Le Surnaturel et la Nature dans la Mentalité primitive* (Paris, 1931).

of the long history of "secularization" is in fact to be found in the Bible?[4]

One might wonder whether it is not a concern here of the theologian rather than the sociologist or even the historian, even if the idea is considered plausible that the conjunction of biblical thought and Greek thought constituted a determinant factor in the evolution of the West.

In fact, until a rationality was discovered in the functioning of the cosmos and in the social processes, Christianity took over the function of the religious guarantor of the social order and of the symbolics of the traditional religions. It played this part in the Roman Empire by taking the place of the system of legitimation and constitution of the collective symbolics of the traditional religions. It managed to survive as a cultural system in a new society which was thus constructed, through different circumstances, on a fundamentally identical pattern.

One might wonder, with Peter Berger, why the religions furnish a system of legitimation. The main function of this is to maintain the cohesion of a society. Historically, Berger affirms, religion has been the most common and effective instrument of legitimation because it connects the precarious construction of social reality to an ultimate reality.[5] But, more profoundly, within the framework of a homogeneity of nature and of society, legitimation can only be religious. This is what one could call an order of total sacrality: recourse to the divine is the determinant element of the system of legitimation of natural and social mechanisms.

With the Renaissance, the functional laws of the universe were precisely defined. This discovery demanded that the natural world be removed from the zone of influence or an immanent deity. It was prepared by the method of Thomist philosophy,

[4] This is affirmed by Arend Th. van Leeuwen in his book *Christianity and World History, The Meeting of the Faiths of East and West* (Edinburgh, 1964). According to this author, all the great civilizations of the East were "ontocratic", i.e., based on a vision of the universe as "cosmic totality". The Bible is the only place in which this conception is rejected, in favour of a theocracy. Greek thought likewise emancipated man from this conception, but in quite a different way. It is in the Judaeo-Christian tradition that the origin is to be found of the process of secularization which permitted the blossoming of Western civilization.

[5] Peter Berger, *op. cit.*, p. 35.

which restored Aristotelian scientific perspectives. It was rooted
in the biblical tradition: God is transcendent, he created man
and granted him powers of dominion over nature. Such a discovery was not without its social difficulties, for it undermined
cosmo-sociological integration, the very basis for the functioning
of society. At this level, however, the consequences were to be
slower in emerging. A first breach was opened in the cultural
and social system as a whole, and institutionalized Christianity
which served as its guarantor was to react.

In fact, from this point of view, the principle of causality received a new content: the idea of law. It was no longer a matter
of a normative regulatory disposition, the observance or omission
of which conditions the phenomenon. The idea of scientific law
expresses a constant bond. By entering the culture, this conception rendered impossible a society subjected in its government
to a totality of precepts of divine origin. In such a system, authority was not only guarantor and upholder of the social order,
but truth itself was merely the expression of the social authority.
From the sociological point of view it could be said that in this
system there was a flattening of legitimations and values on
norms: the totality of the system is normative. The legal regulations themselves have a sacral or religious origin.

The new situation was that of a *partial sacrality* governing
only society. The field of legitimation shrank, but at the same
time it was affirmed with more force than ever before. Even
among those who abandoned the religious explanations of nature,
the social function of religious legitimation still seemed necessary. This was the case for Voltaire, for example.

In a second stage only the social processes became the object
of analysis, in particular thanks to historical studies and to the
discovery of other cultures. Reflection on society was separated
from the deductive process characterized by the philosophical
projection of an ideal society, to become the analysis of a process
on the model of the study of natural processes. This attitude
allowed the blossoming of a critical process and thus of a "desacralization" of power and of the whole of social symbolics. It
was a prelude to the social changes which had become necessary
through the parallel transformation of methods of production.

The most fundamental of contemporary social changes are

situated for the most part at the very cross-roads of the passage from a "sacral" society to a "modern" society, in spite of the shifts in history and the immense variety of situations. The possibilities opened up to man in the scientific and technical field offer him new initiatives, especially in the production and exchange of material goods. An intellectual *élite* has brought about a change of values (scientific approach to the universe) which has generated an economic transformation. This in its turn has released a generalized process of cultural and social change. But the rhythm of change has not been parallel. The system of values based on the dependence of man, and not on his autonomy, is crumbling at a faster rate than the social system. Political power corresponds less and less to economic power and its system of religious legitimation is losing its viability.

II. The Church in Social Transformation[6]

In the Western societies and in their colonies, the Church, before the transformation of socio-political systems, disposed of

[6] When we speak of the Church and of its resistance, we are using the wrong terms. In fact a distinction should be made in the institution not only between different functions but also between different social levels. The magisterium and government are exercised by the hierarchy; it is a matter of the definition of the official positions and of the function of authority in the group. The persons to whom these tasks are entrusted form, for historical reasons, a first very accentuated social stratum within the institution. The clergy form the second and the laity a third stratum, although sociologically much more diversified than the first two.

Generally speaking, it is the hierarchy, guardian of the integrity of the institution and thus also of its relations with society, which reacts most vigorously against social change. This is the more frequent as the mutual relation between the religious institution and society has made of the former the guarantor of the latter and vice versa. In such circumstances no critical distance can be taken by the decision-makers of the ecclesial institution with regard to the existing regime, except at the level of secondary norms, and opposition to a new regime becomes fundamental. Most of the time the majority of the clergy react in a parallel way to that of the hierarchy, for the latter functions as reference group, either for religious or social reasons. There is, however, a certain number of cases in which a considerable section of the clergy does not follow the hierarchy, particularly when a marked difference in social origin renders this clergy solidary with a social group and the hierarchy with another. At other times conflicts of values form the basis of differences and here it is really opposing ideas on the role of the Church which are clashing.

a quasi-monopoly on the definition of values and of a total mono-poly on the system of legitimation, i.e., of explanation. In this sense, it was the guarantor of the social system and this is why religious unity was of such importance for political activity. When the Reformation came about, it inevitably led to wars of religion and the political power was granted on to unanimity of religious adherence. The social movements of the Middle Ages took on almost automatically a religious colour and, in many cases, the official Church participated in their repression, whether it was Catholicism, as in the case of the Waldensians, the Cathari, the Albigensians, the Lollards or even the Occitans, or Luther-anism in the repression of the peasants' revolt under Munzer. One could add to this, in the nineteenth century, the repression of the messianic movements of north-east Brazil and, in the twentieth century, that of kibanguism in the Belgian Congo.

The progressive transformation of values or of the cultural system led to the religious defection of individuals and groups exercising a cultural leadership. The Church answered to this with intransigence, one of the forms of this being the Inquisition, for example. Christianity, in its institutional dimension, thus appeared very closely linked with the whole of society. Its mono-poly on the definition of values prevented new values from being expressed. The Church as institution was guarantor of the social system. Its system of legitimation (doctrinal content) showed itself to be bound to the latter. Moreover, there was osmosis be-tween religious language and the justification of power; the latter was delegated by the religious institution (sacring of kings, of knights).

As for the laity, who are closer to the values of society, generally a diver-sity of options is encountered among them just as broad as in society itself. However, the respective weight of these positions is obviously not the same. Ordinarily a considerable section of those considered socio-logically as members of the ecclesial institution will be found in the camp chosen by the hierarchy.

In short, the higher the status of individuals in the internal stratifica-tion, the greater the chance of resistance to social change. Furthermore, the greater the parallelism between ecclesial structures and social struc-tures, the more the reactions of the hierarchy assimilate those of the ruling élite. This is what we have studied in more detail, by means of a certain number of historical and contemporary cases, in a recent work: *The Church and the Revolution* (New York, 1971).

As for the people, they were integrated in the social values through the expedient of the religious institution. The whole of the ritual, for example, expressed the dominant values and helped the people to conform to them by giving them a transcendent meaning.

It was then inevitable in these circumstances that the break-up of the social system entailed a series of consequences for Christianity. Through its justification of the established order, it maintained a type of reference to God which hindered the emancipation of the individual or of a class, which was precisely what the social movements were seeking. The latter battled against all the upholders of the social system, including the religious authorities.

The opposition of the Church as organization to the revolutionary movements was manifested as though the only form of relation between a revealed religion and a cultural and social system were that which had existed under the *Ancien Régime*. Generally, however, the moment the revolutionary movement lost its virulence, the pattern to which the Church tended to return, or at least to refer to, for a possible normalization, was the one it had known previously. This was verified in France, as in Latin America, by the bias of various forms of "restoration".

Resistance to change was strongest in cases where the Church had played a determinant role in the elaboration and the legitimation of the socio-cultural system overthrown. It is also striking to realize how the unconditional acceptance of a social system can pervert moral judgments. This is verified in the pessimistic judgments on the use of violence: an ignorance is ascertained of established violence, because it is legitimized (legalized, to use Max Weber's expression) and, in contrast, a great sensitiveness towards revolutionary violence, which is deprived of legitimacy.

Oppositions were the harsher if the transformations in the social system were justified among those who undertook them by a system of legitimation in contradiction to that of Christianity. For many, atheism is seen as the only form of total contestation to the *Ancien Régime*, the bourgeois society or political and economic colonialism. The transition from a total sacrality to a partial sacrality, then to a rejection of any recourse to the divine to explain the working of nature and of society, would seem to mark the stages of the situation of the Church in socio-cultural evolution.

III. THE INTERNAL SOCIO-CULTURAL SYSTEM OF THE CHURCH

Very early on in its history, from the fourth century, Christianity, which had become the guarantor of the cultural and social systems of Roman society, took on the internal organization of the latter. This was manifested in the juridical system, as in that of the administration or of authority. The symbols of prestige, of titles, of dress, the very buildings revealed the social image with which it identified itself. The fact that Christianity fulfilled this function certainly had some positive results. It ensured the cohesion of European culture for over five hundred years, probably a necessary condition for a totally new cultural system to be able to flourish, and it supplied, at the time of the collapse of the Roman and Byzantine empires, the bases of a continuity in social systems.

But at the same time this identification fixed Christianity into a precise pattern at the level of systems of value and organization. The great theological syntheses of the Middle Ages reinforced, through the very power of their intellectual constructions, the solidity of identification. In short, it was the pattern of a traditional society which formed the foundation of internal ecclesial organization, i.e., that of a sacral society (with a system of authority modelled on an inalterable pyramidal organization, because it is a reflection of divine authority), partitioned (in relatively autonomous and simple units) and segmented (repeating the pattern of organization in a similar way at the various levels or in the different institutions).

There is no doubt that for the Church the Counter-Reformation helped to reinforce this system. The Roman centralization which was emphasized particularly after the Council of Trent gained full strength after Vatican I. It needed Vatican II to introduce the new values officially, i.e., to make them accepted by the system of legitimation of the Church.

During all this period the Church necessarily had to appear as upholding values bound to the existence of a traditional society. It is not surprising that it regularly attracted the conservative social forces and that it felt, as institution, generally closer to such forces than to the forces of change. The moment certain members of the hierarchy assumed attitudes favouring changes in society, these same social sectors manifested opposition or horror. The Church was in effect perceived as guarantor of their social status. In those places where society was stratified in a new way, so that the Church was no longer able to play this role for the whole of the social system, it fulfilled it at least for a section of the latter. This was the case for the bourgeoisie emerging from industrialization, as also for the colonial administrations in Africa and Asia. This was also the case in the developing countries, for the traditional élite or for the new élite of power.

It is striking to see how the cultural pattern of the exercise of authority and of power of the traditional society still seems to underlie bourgeois or colonial societies and the new élite of the countries of the third world. Its permanence throughout social changes explains a certain number of contradictions between the collective attitudes of these élites of power and the explanation they give of democratic society. It is here that the latent function of ideology is grafted on as justification of power. The permanence of this cultural pattern is also verified in the case of the Church as institution. Throughout the events of history, in spite of painful experiences, beyond the legitimation of new positions, the same attitudes re-emerge, bound to a function of guarantor of the traditional society. The theory of the "two societies", still turned to in the plan for reforming canon law, can obviously only lead to the support of the political and social *status quo*.

What we have just said obviously does not take into account all situations, which are often much more complex and nuanced. It is rather a process which has been described and which, under very varied circumstances in the evolution of societies, has also assumed diverse forms. However, the existence of this process allows an understanding of why and to what end extra-ecclesial interests operate for maintaining the *status quo* of the Churches.

This article is merely intended to indicate courses of reflection and research, but also to show that they are not to be sought in simplistic explanations referring solely to immediate events.

Translated by Della Couling

Joseph Comblin

Outside Criticism
of the Church

MISSIONARIES have always encountered criticism from among the peoples they have tried to evangelize. This type of criticism still exists in Asia and Africa. But there is a difference between the accusations levelled at the Church in places where a complex and elaborated religion already exists, capable of resisting the cultural pressure of the West, and the accusations encountered in places where the more primitive local religions are incapable of offering effective resistance.

The former case is that of the great religions of the East: there is a close similarity between the objections made against the Christian Churches in Japan, China, India, South-East Asia and the Arab world.

First of all, the Churches are reproached with their contempt for the great religions of the East and with their sense of superiority. The proselytism of the Christian missions has completely disregarded the traditional religions. The Christians have demanded quite simply of the Orientals that they abandon their traditional wisdom to adopt a new religion imported wholesale. This is considered an insult.

Secondly, the missions are accused of having accepted or even sought the support of the colonizers: thus they have shown themselves to be accessory to colonial aggression. Furthermore, they have profited from the humiliation of the traditional *élite* to buy the support of the poor and the illiterate, sometimes by pretty low methods, such as material advantages, and they have trained these masses, with the support of the colonial powers, against the culture and religion of their own country.

Furthermore, the cultural colonialism engaged in by the Churches is denounced. Through their institutions of education, health, assistance, their social and other organizations, all copied from the West, they have made themselves, it is said, propagandists of Western culture under the pretext of evangelizing. Abusing the prestige of the Gospel, they have introduced cultural values from the West and thus created new needs which inevitably render the traditional cultures dependent on the Western countries which produce these values.

Finally, to the degree in which Orientals become aware of the divisions in the Christian Church and the conflicts which, even in the West, set it against secularized culture, the missions are reproached with having introduced among foreign peoples new conflicts which they could well have done without.

The criticisms of the Church made among the peoples of more primitive culture are even graver. It is mainly a matter of the work of the missions among the American Indians or in Black Africa. It is here most of all that the missionaries have played the role of intermediaries between Western culture and the primitive clans or tribes. Believing they were teaching them Christianity, they compelled them to adopt customs which were merely Western and which destroyed the balance of their society. In this way, the missions destroyed the powers of resistance of the peoples they helped to conquer. They rendered them defenceless against exploitation, poverty, even genocide, in many parts of the American continent, for example. Believing, no doubt, in all good faith, that they were opening the way for them to the "benefits" of civilization, in the end they merely opened up access to its drawbacks: the survivors of these primitive peoples are now crowded into shanty-towns, at the gates of a world whose mechanisms they do not understand.

The criticisms of catechesis are particularly severe. It is through catechesis, they say, that the Church has destroyed the soul of the peoples. It has done away with the cohesion and balance of the traditional beliefs without replacing them with any coherent message, for the scraps of Christian doctrine the American Indians and blacks have managed to pick up do not form an intelligible whole. The primitive peoples have lost their self-consciousness and are seeking desperately to reassemble the pieces of their former philosophy, together with what they can understand of the new messages. They are powerless to tackle the great disputes of Western culture into which the mission introduced them, unwittingly perhaps. Some even go so far as to say that catechesis has done more to destroy the primitive peoples than political or economic domination (see the criticisms of Cl. Lévi-Strauss).

II. "Post-Christian" Criticism

Another type of criticism has emerged in the West. It can be called post-Christian criticism because it is the product of individuals who were born and grew up within the Church, or at least in a world permeated by its influence. These people by no means wish to destroy the contribution of the Church; they merely wish to pass beyond it. They believe the Church was able to orient and form the West up to a certain point in its evolution, but that it must now yield. Better still, some even go so far as to say that it is the Church itself which taught the principles allowing it to be overtaken today. It is interesting to note that Nazism, which intended to efface the influence of Christianity and somehow return, by-passing Christianity, to the sources of Germanic paganism, was only an aberrant moment in contemporary history, and that it does not seem to have left important traces. On the other hand, the fundamental criticism of the Church seeks to pass beyond Christianity.

The history of post-Christian criticism of the Church is full of lessons. In the era of the Enlightenment, the Church was above all reproached with maintaining the people under the yoke of a "positive" religion. By so doing, it was said, the Church hindered the development of the "natural" religion, which answered the demands of reason, of science and of progress. Through the preaching of its priests and its ignorant monks, the Church kept alive in the masses prejudices, superstition, absurd customs. The more ignorant the masses remained, the more they supplied the Church with troops of workers which the clergy knew how to handle to preserve its privileges and requisition the use of the secular arm. Under these conditions, criticism of the Church was a holy war, a crusade for the liberation of the people from the yoke of ignorance; to battle against the Church was to battle for science, for reason, for the emancipation of the people dominated by the power of the priests and the power of the kings, closely bound and solidary.

The criticisms of the Enlightenment waned at the same time as the influence of the Church in society. But they are still sometimes found in the Iberian peninsula and in Latin America, where critics denounce the attachment of the clergy to an archaic society and their opposition to social revolution: the Church keeps its social prestige there thanks to the ignorance of the rural masses. Moreover, even in the most developed countries, the fact is pointed out that by mustering the last remnants of medieval Europe in its mass organizations, and by protecting them from any critical spirit, the Catholic Church has been able to win back a status of semi-official Church, endowed with many privileges partly endorsed under the cover of so-called "lay" or secularized Constitutions.

In the name of liberalism, the nineteenth century popularized the criticisms of the century of Enlightenment. But it also bred a new and much more radical form of criticism, aimed this time at the very foundations of the Church, i.e., at religion and the idea of God. Feuerbach, Marx, Nietzsche and, later, Freud are the most representative authors of the classical criticism of religion and of classical atheism.

Classical criticism of religion is presented as a work of demystification. It undertakes the task of liberating man and creating a true humanism by tearing away the veil of religious illusion. It too had a crusading spirit about it and a revolutionary enthusiasm. According to it, God and religion are the alienation of man. God is a projection of man outside himself, and religion is a compensation in an existence diminished through lack of power or of the will to live a truly human life.

This criticism endeavoured to be universal and was aimed at all religion. In fact, the religion it described was Christianity— Christianity such as was taught and actually lived in the Churches. For example, the religion denounced by Marx was the popular Christianity which the Churches carefully cultivated under the protection of the very pious monarchies of the Restoration, that popular Christianity whose anti-revolutionary virtues the rising bourgeoisie very quickly came to appreciate. Likewise, the death of God which Nietzsche proclaimed he ascertained in the Christianity of his time. Religious infantilism and its repressive legalism were ascertained by Freud among his Viennese patients and he attributed them to their religion.

Hence the work of demystification of classical atheism is not aimed at metaphysical entities: its aim is to destroy the religious idea in the place where it is cultivated—in the Christian Church.

The classical criticism of religion was broadly popularized during the first half of the twentieth century. At the moment it is losing momentum. Although it is still the official doctrine in the Communist countries, militant atheism has ceased to be a dominant of Western culture. The present-day criticism of religion is situated beyond atheism; radical criticism of religion has been transformed into a radical criticism of all culture, of all institutions and of all objectivation. The revolution has become a general contestation of the West and indeed of all humanism. Beyond religion, it is ascertained that humanism is already an alienation: just as much as God, man is myth or ideology (structuralism). However, the extreme radicalization of this criticism suggests its own limits: if demystified man ceases to exist, then a certain value must be restored to the mystifications, and the myth recovers its rights.

Another factor has contributed to attenuating the aggressiveness of the classical criticism: the advent of the human sciences. A sociology or psychology of the criticism of religion can be applied just as well as a sociology or psychology of religion itself. Under these conditions, criticism of religion becomes reflexive: it studies itself as one of the phenomena of the history of religions and a type of religious attitude. Thanks to the scientific perspective, criticism of religion is becoming as relative as religion. Present-day criticism is critical to the second degree.

Finally, many have acquired the conviction that the Churches have been definitively eliminated from social life, which permits people to regard them with more tolerance. This impression marks public opinion in such a way that a new integrism has been born among Christians to cry out from the roof-tops that

God is not dead, that they met him in the street and that it is not true what is being said.

In the second half of the twentieth century indifference has succeeded atheism. The problem of God has become obsolete. Consequently the Church has become uninteresting. The need to criticize it is no longer felt. When objections are voiced against the Church, it is in answer to the questions of Christians. The criticisms are reasons given to justify one's indifference. These are no longer attacks, they are possible responses to the solicitations of Christians.

In the face of this development, the attitude of the Churches has changed too. When the Churches occupied positions of power side by side with the princes, they sought out criticisms in an inquisitorial spirit to track down heresy, denounce it or draw down upon it the repression of the ecclesiastical tribunals or of the secular arm. When the State became secularized, it was attempted to keep the bulk of the people shielded from the criticisms of "naturalism", "rationalism" or "liberalism". Theologians took up criticisms as objections to be refuted. They composed an immense apologetic literature which never succeeded in convincing any "adversary" but the efficacy of which consisted in reassuring the faithful. The apologists willingly cited the objections of unbelievers to show that the Church had an answer to everything, and that good people could find safe shelter in this impregnable fortress.

Apologetics died at the same time as the aggressive criticisms of the last century. Today it has been ascertained that a worse thing is indifference. The theologians beseech unbelievers to be kind enough to formulate objections. They are invited to collaborate in theological commentaries. These criticisms are thankfully received for they are put to the account of the "pathology" of the Church. By means of criticism, it is hoped to free the Church from its deficiencies or from its excessive compromises with cultures or social groups. Instead of rejecting criticism, the tendency is to integrate it into a truly dialectical attitude.

After this quick sketch of the history of post-Christian criticism, let us take a look at the present situation: firstly, what remains of classical criticism, and then what are the reasons given to justify indifference.

III. The Present State of Classical Criticism

Classical atheism and the classical criticism of religion did not break the Churches. On the contrary, the latter succeeded in assimilating them. Theology integrated them, to cause the emergence of what is called secularization. All things considered, the theology of secularization is the clearest result of atheism. Those most interested in atheism are the theologians.

This is why, just as neo-Marxism must take into account the triumphs of neo-capitalism, neo-atheism renews itself by taking into account the theology of secularization. The latter obliges it to make distinctions and to nuance arguments. The present-day disciples of Marx, of Freud or of Nietzsche have tried to nuance the religious criticism of their masters, by showing that it does not apply to all aspects of the Church indiscriminately.

In the first place, the classical criticism denounces projections of man beyond man in religious representations. The independent Marxists of today acknowledge, according to E. Bloch and R. Garaudy, with the Italian or Yugoslav parties, that this criticism does not affect secularized theology to the degree in which the latter draws out and develops the immanence of God in man. They take note of the theology of the world of Teilhard de Chardin and of the distinction between faith and religion of D. Bonhoeffer. Marxist criticism was aimed more at religion than faith. Likewise, the disciples of Freud suggest that the explanations of the Viennese master are more a pathology of Christianity than a universally valid interpretation.

Under these conditions, the Church is now being accused of ambiguity and of not making a choice between two theologies, which makes it look as though it were decisively resisting taking the part of man.

Secondly, the classical criticism of religion acknowledges the Church a provisional and limited function. The religious projection plays a role in the formation of the conscience. It need only become obsolete when it ceases to be naïve. Modern criticisms insist particularly on this positive aspect of religion, and on the contribution of the Church to civilization. Some Marxists point out that even in socialist society the Church will still be able to play a role until the new man appears: there will still be the problem of death, of the person and of love, problems for which socialism will not find immediate solutions. Likewise the Freudians insist on the civilizing role of religion.

The third point of the classical criticism consists in denouncing the institutional apparatus of the Church, which tends to exist for its own sake and be an aim in itself. These institutions consider themselves absolute and mobilize the energy of believers in their service. Thus they hinder the self-awareness of man by regarding him as means to an extra-human end. Now here too we note the criticism of the dualism of Christianity; of the influence of ecclesiastical apparatus and bureaucracy, as can be found in the Church of today. It has been pointed out that the idea of service was promoted by Vatican II and by *Populorum Progressio*; the Church is accused of not being consistent with its own principles. The Church continues to have only its own interests in view. It can be said with Merleau-Ponty: The Church has never been known to take the part of a revolution just because the revolution was just. On the other hand, it has always been known to be ready to bless the arms of those who defended its privileges (i.e., the Spanish civil war, or the declaration of Pius XI on Mexico). The Church subordinates its support, in social or international struggles, to the imperatives, considered supreme, of the anti-Communism of the bourgeoisie (thus it fights for the rearmament of Germany, but against the Latin-American revolutions).

Finally, the classical criticism accuses the Churches of transforming themselves into instruments of domination by assuming the ideology of the capitalist system. Here again, modern critics recognize secularized theology's refutation of Constantinian Christianity, as also of the social therapy of the modern individualizing of religion. Present-day Marxists take up Engels' distinction between Judaic or apocalyptic Christianity, which is the expression of an aspiration to freedom, and Greek or Constantinian Christianity which was merely the ideology of imperial domination. But they accuse the modern Church of not choosing between its revolutionary principle (E. Bloch, P. Togliatti) and its solidarities with established systems. The Church continues to impose its own interests on the whole nation, especially on the subject of the family, education and health or assistance. Its theology of the just war, of private property and of the social order serves it to recognize violence when it has triumphed, but not to take sides for justice when the issue is uncertain. In short, the Church is accused of being Machiavellian.

IV. THE REASONS FOR INDIFFERENCE

Of all the criticisms of the last century, the most relevant for today is that of Nietzsche. The young have grown away from the Church because they feel there is nothing more to be expected of it. They ascertain that it has played no part in the great victories of humanity in recent centuries, that it plays no part in the dynamism of the modern world. They conclude from this that it has no future. They find that Christians themselves no longer take their faith seriously. It seems to them that Christianity as a faith is dead. What remains is religiosity among the elderly or adults in distress, and a bureaucratic apparatus which profits by this religiosity to maintain economic and social positions. Nothing more. The problem of the Church no longer arises. When the young are asked to list their objections, they reply as follows.

In the first place, there is the spectacle offered by the Church in its visible institutions: hierarchy, colleges, universities, social movements and organizations. The Church seems bound to its medieval or baroque past. It speaks the language of its past. It seems to expect the world to return to it. It has no future plan to propose to the world. It has been absent from the liberation movements which have been the soul of history over recent centuries. It ends up by rallying to the victories of liberty, but always behindhand and reluctantly, as it were. When new movements of emancipation appear, the Church is quick to point out the dangers and excesses threatening from them, without feeling solidary. For the young, the mere fact of having nothing to suggest but a return to the Church of one's forefathers is enough grounds for considering Christianity outdated.

In the second place, the demystified man of today, who has himself demystified atheism, cannot take seriously a Church which shows itself to be pre-critical in its doctrine, its morals and its social system. The dogma jealously defended by the

Church is inassimilable. How can it interest the man of today that formerly an act of creation took place, then that there was a sin, the consequences of which, however, have been effaced by a redemption? What interest can there be in seeking to have such a message admitted? As for morals, they give the impression of being merely the maintenance of the prohibitions of the traditional rural society, especially of its sexual prohibitions. The young have the impression that the Church features in their lives only in the form of sexual taboos. Finally, the hierarchy presiding over this system is an anguished gerontocracy jealous of its prerogatives. In short, everything contributes to the impression of being merely a system with no other ambition but to survive.

The opinion of the average Catholic confirms this impression. In fact, the average Catholic is a being frightened by the evolution of modern man. He lacks ease and assurance. He has neither the sense nor the use of freedom. He is someone who cannot judge for himself and must always refer to his Church to know what he must think or do. The Catholic is someone who cannot do this, that and the other. He is a limited being. And he fanatically defends his limits. He is intolerant and hotly defends his dogmas, as also his taboos and his institutions. For all this, "Catholics are worth no more than others". Hence, what is the good of being Christian?

Finally, what alienates the Church is its particularism. To be Christian is to limit oneself. The non-Christian has the impression of being more open to the universal man, while the Church makes man more determinate and particular.

The Church is not really interested in others. It regards them as sick to be cared for or forces to be conquered. It turns men into instruments. It does not seek change, for it does not believe it needs it. Its dialogue is merely tactics. Religious liberty is for the Church merely a protection against interference from the State, but it does not hold within the Church itself. In short, the Church has succeeded in gaining a place in present-day society, but it is the place of a private society with particular interests: it looks after the needs of the religiosity of the victims of the system, for the same reasons as Moral Rearmament or the Rotary Club. This is why the Church does not take up the point of view of the universal man, but the point of view of its particular (religious) interests.

As can be seen, criticism is by no means directed at the theoretical idea of the Church as taught in the official documents. It is a matter here of the actual Church as it is lived by those it recognizes as its own and who claim to be such.

Translated by Della Couling

Heinz Schlette

On so-called "Partial Identification" with the Church

"Sentire cum Ecclesia"—this can demand from us that we break with Catholicism as it is today.[1] It is a statement that points to a conflict which has almost always existed in the history of the Church. There can be no doubt that this conflict is once again with us, and in more accentuated form. We have long known that a considerable number of Christians, even "members of the Church", no longer participate at all, or only to a limited degree, in what is loosely called the "life of the Church". Statistical questions about the total number of those who are no longer "practising" or fully practising, or of those who believe the Church's teaching in its entirety, or only part of it, are probably impossible to answer with exactitude. Though it is true that inquiries more far-reaching than the customary counting of heads at Eastertide have for years been made in some of the European countries at least. But this is something else again.

I. CHARACTERISTIC FEATURES OF THE PROBLEM

In the most recent past attempts have been made, by means of the concept of "partial identification", to come to grips with the problem of those who belong to the Church and yet do not "totally identify" with it, and to re-think this problem by means of a fundamental reappraisal of the nature of the Church and the

[1] C. Amery, *Die Kapitulation oder Deutscher Katholizismus heute* (Reinbek b. Hamburg, 1963), p. 117 (Eng. trans. *Capitulation: An Analysis of Contemporary Catholicism*, London, 1967).

possibilities within it.[2] Up to the present time our understanding of the Church was such that the concept of "total identification" presented no problems. Indeed such identification was seen as exacting, in the name of God and Jesus, complete submission to the teachings of the Church and the commands of the central authority at Rome—a submission, moreover, that included the inner assent of the conscience. This interpretation of "Church", "life of the Church", "practising Catholics" was in accord with the exclusively negative and pejorative description (by the totally participating) of those who only "partially identified" as "paper Catholics", "fringe Christians", "Christians asleep", "luke-warm" or "dead" Christians.

The new thinking on the Church by Rahner and Metz is not of course intended to give retrospective theological respectability to certain clearly deplorable forms of "partial identification" such as religious indifference, dubious popular customs and ignorance. Such an attempt would merely be to idealize a defective disposition and would thus be meaningless. Moreover, it would not stand up in face of the unequivocal demands made by the Bible for man's "heart", his total love, total self-giving. Nevertheless the fact of partial identification is interesting, for several reasons. It leads us, at any rate in the first instance, to look for a cause of this phenomenon elsewhere than in the moral behaviour of so-called "bad Christians" and the apathy of the good; to examine self-critically the whole concrete and structural pattern and reality of a Church that demands from us "total identification" (see section II).

The results of such an analysis could bring greater understanding for the "dialectics" of identification as a whole. Indeed it already seems as though we must abandon our old understanding of "total identification" and come to see "partial identification" as the necessary precondition for true life in and with the Church, the only possible, only "true" identification to which we can commit ourselves (see section III). These two problems will be considered in the following pages. But I am well aware that what I am giving is only an outline sketch.

[2] J. B. Metz, *Reform und Gegenreformation heute* (Mainz, 1969), pp. 29 f. Cf. also K. Rahner, "Schisma in der Katholischen Kirche?", in *Schriften zur Theologie*, IX (Einsiedeln–Zürich–Cologne, 1970), pp. 448–52.

II. Review of the Pattern of "Total Identification"

The concept of "total identification" is rooted in the traditional and still widely disseminated dogmatic, juridical, spiritual and pastoral teaching of the Church.

The question of adherence to the Church, membership of the Church, is basically one of dogma and Church law.[3] The problem of full and true membership of the Church is, as Karl Rahner insists, no other than the problem of the true "nature" of the Church.[4] It implies, at any rate as regards dogma, the question of the indirect membership, or "relationship", to the Church of non-Catholic Christians and non-Christians as a whole (cf. *Lumen Gentium*, nn. 13, 15 and 16). I should like to refer at this point to the well-known discussions concerning the ecclesial character of the non-Catholic Christian communions[5] and to the theories about "anonymous Christianity",[6] the "latent Church"[7] and "structural Christianity".[8] But I must confine my own thesis to what constitutes explicit membership of the Roman Catholic Church, as the Church itself has stated it.

The encyclical *Mystici Corporis* of Pius XII (1943) says that membership of the Church is in actual fact (*reapse*) confined to those who have been re-born in the waters of baptism, who confess the true faith, have not separated themselves from the Body to their own detriment, nor been excluded from it by rightful authority on account of their own grievous sins (Denz. 3802). This is followed by a discussion of the meaning of the concepts *membrum* and *persona* (cf. CIC can. 87) and whether or in what

[3] It is not possible to consider here the extent to which dogma and Church law are identical in this context.

[4] Cf. K. Rahner, "Kirchengliedschaft (Kirchenzugehörigkeit)", in *Sacramentum Mundi—Theologisches Lexikon für die Praxis*, II (Freiburg–Basle–Vienna).

[5] Cf. A. Grillmeier, on *Lumen Gentium*, chapter II, n. 15, in *Lthk—Das Zweite Vatikanische Konzil*, I (1966), pp. 200–05; J. Feiner, "On the Decree on Ecumenism, chapter I", in *ibid.*, II (1967), pp. 44–49.

[6] Cf. now K. Rahner, "Anonymes Christentum und Missionsauftrag der Kirche", in *Schriften zur Theologie*, IX, *loc. cit.*, pp. 498–515.

[7] Cf. P. Tillich, "Offenbarung und Glaube", in *Schriften zur Theologie*. II (collected works VIII) (Stuttgart, 1970), pp. 276–84.

[8] Cf. H. R. Schlette, "Struckturen des Christentums, philosophisch", in *Aporie und Glaube, Schriften zur Philosophie und Theologie* (Munich, 1970), pp. 102–21.

degree excommunication destroys or diminishes membership of the Church.[9] The Council Constitution *Lumen Gentium* once again returns to this theme but avoids the word *"membra"* and distinguishes between "full" incorporation (*"plene"*, cf. n. 14) and the different forms of relationship (cf. nn. 13, 15 and 16). According to n. 14 there are three, or as it may be four, binding conditions for full membership—profession of faith, the sacraments (without further qualification) and the obligation of *"ecclesiastici regiminis ac communionis"*. We note, too, the explicit reference to the distinction between membership of the heart, *"corde"*, and (only) of the body, *"corpore"*. This distinction receives additional validity from a text in Augustine which also contains the famous double concept of *"intus-foris"*.[10]

It may be sufficient to remind ourselves here that the dogmatic and juridical approach to the question of Church membership leads to a concept of identification that is one-sided, immobilist, ontological and institutional. Actual, concrete identification, even if only partial and therefore deficient, retains a negative ecclesiastical significance, in so far as it plays a part in the field of moral and pastoral theology. But a man's real position within the Church, his so to say empirically significant "status", does not touch in any way on dogma or Church law. These spring direct from revelation, from divine truth and divine law, and thus induce an attitude which, if it is to be considered totally, that is to say "fully" identified with the Church (a necessary condition for salvation, subjectively speaking—cf. *Lumen Gentium*, n. 14)— must be based on an authoritarian view of obedience and loyalty. Only total identification with the concrete will of the Church as expressed by the ecclesiastical and hierarchical authority, will produce the ideal Catholic or the idea of the ideal Catholic or, to put it differently, the ascetic and spiritual ideal of "holiness" or "perfection".

We need not describe in detail how the requirements of total identification are channelled and delegated from Pope to bishops, to vicars general, heads of seminaries, superiors of religious orders

---

[9] Cf. K. Rahner's detailed treatise on "Die Gliedschaft in der Kirche nach der Lehre der Enzyklika Pius' XII, *Mystici Corporis Christi*", in *Schriften zur Theologie*, II, *loc. cit.* (1957), pp. 7–94.

[10] Cf. A. Grillmeier, *loc. cit.*, pp. 198–200.

and even parish priests and chaplains, in a diffusion of light and power that resembles the neo-Platonic—a mode of thought that is still very much with us.

In these circumstances all attempts to relax, reform or even change this radial power system by means of the "ultimately everything depends on God" idea are bound to be regarded, at the beginning, as "disturbances", the agitations of heretics who are trying to introduce perplexities and uncertainties into what is a God-given "order". In the pastoral, moral and theological view, these "disturbances" are of necessity suspect, and are frequently condemned as disobedience, arrogance, rebelliousness, and so on.[11]

The history of the conflicts that have arisen from such confrontations has not yet been written. A beginning might be made with the confrontation between Peter and Paul (Gal. 2. 11). If we confine ourselves to the most significant examples, we could also cite the names of Peter Abelard, Francis of Assisi and Meister Eckhart, from the Middle Ages. The post-Syllabus Modernist period, moreover, and the period following the already legendary Second Vatican Council, would provide ample additional scope for research. This would reveal, among other things and despite all expectations to the contrary and the demands made by total identification, the positive, reformist and inspirational character of most "disturbances", even the heretical. Omitting them, it would not be possible truthfully to describe or comprehend the Church's passage through the centuries.

But just as we cannot assert that all canonized saints have been "reformers" (for clearly there have been "conservative" saints too), so we cannot stand the thesis upside down and insist that those who criticized and disrupted the old order were always "reformers" and never the conservative "orthodox". Clearly the entire spectrum of human attitudes is present in the Church as elsewhere.

Fortunately we are beginning to understand now about the existence of different views within the Church and the notion of tolerance. We are beginning not only to practise these virtues in

[11] Cf. W. Rohrer, "Leben heisst: Gestört werden", in *Orientierung*, 34 (1970), pp. 117–19.

the area of morality, but to give them a firm basis in the institutional structure of the Church. An exclusively moral response to these problems is not possible. An invitation to the individual to improve matters by first improving himself would be utopian and ineffective.

In other words—we are just beginning to recognize possible deficiencies in the idea of total identification, and to acquire a new understanding of the concept of partial identification. But before we can pursue these questions here, we must once again refer to the negative forms of partial identification in order to avoid certain misunderstandings.

The modern world has seen profound changes in the historical scene and these, together with the accompanying and increasingly sharp criticisms of religion, Christianity and Church, have been the occasion of conflicts that have made it more and more difficult to believe at all[12]—quite apart from the fact that Europe has had no religious alternative to Christianity. If we examine the sum total of these modern anti-Christian criticisms, the weight of the arguments contained in them and the strength of the feelings involved, we shall not be surprised that the idea of total identification has become an empty dream. And we shall have to admit, for good or ill, that all forms of partial identification— up to and including the very smallest—deserve a certain acceptance if we compare them with the all too likely possibility of the disappearance of the idea of identification altogether.

In saying this I do not in any way wish to attack the convinced atheist or agnostic. On the other hand I am not, when it comes down to it, able to countenance certain forms of degenerate "bourgeois" environmental Christianity. It seems to me important, in view of keeping the account straight and taking note of those who still remain despite the attacks of modern critics, to judge the situation calmly and dispassionately.

If of course we consider the dubious reputation of this form of partial identification, if we look at the malleability of this kind of "Christian people" and the perpetual compromise of things Christian that is the result of such a view, and to some extent inspired the critical attitude of Asians and Africans, if we study

---

[12] Cf. the still impressive presentation of this theme in the novel *Jean Barois* by Robert Martin du Gard (1913).

the well-known criticisms of the Church of Voltaire, Kant, Marx and then of Nietzsche, Russell, Camus, Sartre, and so on, then we are faced with the question of whether it would not be best, for the Gospel's sake, to discard this kind of dead weight altogether. It is this very question which once again confronts us with an inescapable ambivalence. Is it not precisely a certain form of *total* identification that has been called in question by the modern critics, the total identification of those formal and paper Christians who are officially orthodox, but whose immobilism, whose lack of human uprightness, has called down on them the near-universal protests of those outside, and also from time to time those inside, the Church? It is not possible to determine the measure of participation, let alone responsibility, of those who partially or those who totally identify. We may be content to leave this problem and now turn exclusively to the question of the degree to which partial identification has both a positive and a necessary function for the Church.

III. Partial Identification as the Precondition for the Possibility of True Identification

The ideas contained in the heading to this section may at first glance seem surprising and strange. We shall show, however, the sense in which these ideas are not merely theologically representative (perhaps even in the context of a certain "bad" pluralist theology that permits everything and no longer recognizes the idea of deviation[13]), but are in accord with a fundamental theological necessity without which the Church cannot be what it is supposed to be.

The concept of partial identification lays claim to a reality that cannot be evaded by calling on any kind of dogmatic or juridical principle. We have already shown how illuminating the concept of partial identification is in itself, and how various the causes that have brought and continue to bring it to the foreground. We may speak of partial identification entered into involuntarily in the course of religious practice, but also of a deliberately

[13] Cf. K. Rahner, "Häresien in der Kirche heute", in *Schriften zur Theologie*, IX, *loc. cit.*, pp. 453–78. See also H. Küng, *Unfehlbar? Eine Anfrage* (Zürich–Einsiedeln–Cologne, 1970), esp. pp. 116–96.

chosen partial identification. In the latter case the very delibera-
tion of one's choice is an indication of the measure of distance
and estrangement involved, but on the other hand also of the
gravity of a greater loyalty which can only be articulated—help-
lessly enough—by means of distance, refusal, disobedience, and
perhaps even protest. What is interesting here is not so much the
empirically exact psychology of partial identifications in matters
of religion and belief, but the basic attitude of the Church as
regards the positive and necessary character of such partial identification. Thus we shall concentrate on the second and deliberately chosen mode of partial identification, to which we have just
referred. For we must have no illusion about the great majority
of those who can still be said to partially identify, though to an
extent difficult to determine qualitatively, whether implicitly or
explicitly, in an attitude of negative scepticism. It looks as though
only a relatively small number of those who are not practising
or only practising in a limited way, can be won over to a new,
positive, reformist mode of partial identification.

In section II of this essay, à propos of the problem of Church
membership, we showed how there existed and continues to exist
in the Church the ideal of total identification as the natural consequence of an obvious and dangerous identification of the claims
of God and the Church. But now we have to show that the idea
of total identification, however orthodox it may appear, can only
be regarded as theologically absurd. This verdict is in no sense
too severe. It necessarily emerges from the traditional thinking
of the Church, and also from its practice. For it is the needs of
the latter that have stimulated the theological ideas which have
for long stood in opposition to the dubious concept of total identification. Here I can only give a brief summary of the theological
data. I am not able to deal with the totality of dogmatic, moral-
theological, pastoral and even mystical questions that are involved.

We begin by reminding ourselves of the traditional teaching
about conscience, which was not of course invented by Thomas
Aquinas. This teaching implies—if we are to be consistent—the
permanent and unchanging obligation of critical alertness, despite
all attempts to subordinate the Christian conscience to the
Church's teaching office. Our responsibility before God, whom

we must obey more than man, cannot be so manipulated and delegated that it shrinks to a responsibility to the hierarchy. It may be that in practice an individual prefers to let himself be instructed by the hierarchy (especially as the latter has the right and duty, to an extent we cannot discuss here, to teach and defend the demands made by the Christian life). But in essence the interpretations of the hierarchy are not *ipso facto* identical with the binding demands of the will of God. Thomas Aquinas's teaching about conscience makes this perfectly clear. If we were to confine this principle to exceptional cases only, to those wiser and better informed and skilful enough to know how to manipulate the rules in their own favour, then we should rightly be accused of pastoral cynicism and a contempt for man that has nothing in common with the liberating and humanizing intentions of Jesus and would invalidate every rightful command of a rational humanity.

Clearly the Church's teaching on conscience must be the basis for whatever criticisms we make of the concept of total identification. But other theological realities enter into it too, in particular prophecy and charismata. No prophet or charismatic has ever, prior to his public emergence, allowed himself to be given official sanction to criticize or experiment. It is true that the Church alone claims the right to discern spirits authentically and to judge of the legitimacy and orthodoxy of prophets and charismatics. But this official discernment of spirits is necessarily preceded by another, freer, charismatic discernment which cannot be evaded —in other words by a form of partial identification that postulates the right to criticize Church affairs and to make additions and alterations to them.

The principle of the "discernment of spirits" is thus opposed to the view of total identification and justifies an attitude of legitimate disobedience[14] for the sake of true adherence to God and Jesus—a disobedience which, dialectically and ironically speaking, can be thought of as "anticipatory obedience", in so far as it relates to a new and better practice in the Church, but which, at root, is also the "material" disobedience of merely partial identification.

[14] Cf. H. R. Schlette, "Früchte des Ungehorsams", in *Kirche unterwegs* (Theologia publica 3) (Olten–Freiburg, 1966), pp. 61-7.

This then is the theological as well as the juridical basis for the introduction of new usages, new customs and new practices in the Church. Indeed the faith of the Christian people (cf. 1 Peter 2. 9) must constantly refer back to the driving force behind that faith, and because it is a faith springing from the Holy Spirit, must aim to produce new utterances and introduce new usages and new practices. These will at first necessarily be in opposition to the old.

"Sentire cum Ecclesia"[15]—thinking in accord with the inner mind of the Church—cannot simply be defined as *"sentire cum hierarchia"*, because the hierarchy is not the Church, and the Church is no unchanging but only a temporal entity, for it is not the kingdom of God. Thinking with the Church is only possible from a position of deliberately chosen distance, not from one of total identification that leaves no room for new life, new breath and new development. It is precisely in the "Catholic", indeed the Ignatian, principle of *"sentire cum Ecclesia"* that we can clearly see how total identification, based of necessity upon authority and obedience, *status quo* and order, is nothing other than death by suffocation. The free play of the imagination,[16] on the other hand, that seeks to identify itself with the inner meaning of the Church and strives for a *"sentire cum Ecclesia"* in this sense, can only occur through partial identification. Thus we have here a negation of a negation within the Church, a momentary ecclesiastical dialectic. Partial identification is the precondition for the possibility of true identification with the Church, but *true* identification is not "total" identification. This sentence, alas, is very far from being a play upon words.

In his technological, political, utopian novel *We* (1920), E. Zamyatin invented a space-craft which he called "Integral". He intended the name to be a reflection of the absolute claims made by a totalitarian state that cynically gives itself out to be a benefactor, and demands total identification. The novel quotes a newspaper article that depressingly ends thus:

... You are sick. Your sickness is called imagination. The imagination is a worm that digs black furrows in your brow,

[15] Cf. H. Wulf, "Sentire cum Ecclesia", in *Lthk²*, IX, pp. 674 f.
[16] Cf. D. Solle, *Phantasie und Gehorsam*. Überlegungen zu einer künftigen christlichen Ethik (Stuttgart–Berlin, 1968).

a fever that drives you on ever faster though it only begins where happiness comes to an end. Imagination is the last obstacle on the path to happiness.

Be glad that this obstacle has been set aside.

The way is free.

National scientific research has recently made an important discovery. The centre of the imagination is lodged in a tiny area at the base of the brain. Irradiate the spot three times, and you are healed of your imagination. For ever.

You are perfect, you are like machines, the way is free for perfect happiness. Come to the operating theatres for your operations. Long live the big operation, long live the single state! Long live the benefactor![17]

The vision of such a state (which has also been described by Huxley, Orwell and others) is the vision of total identification. But when applied to the Church, it is even more terrible. A Church in which imagination is an illness to be got rid of, a Church as "Integral", would be no less a form of destructive death and negating nothingness than the Moloch state of Zamyatin. "Integrated communities" are dead communities.

But we happily assert, and with greater justice, that the Church possesses not a few characteristics that could save it from a stifling integration—though it is true that total identification seems to many a worthy aim and the necessary, but perhaps also the more comfortable, attitude. It must actually seem paradoxical and ironic at the same time when, more or less explicitly in the name of total identification, those who partially identify see their freedom as the precondition for the possibility of reform and are then made to understand they are no longer orthodox. In this context J. B. Metz was right to underline the orthodoxy of the reformer.[18]

We can simplify the problem only if we reduce it to sociological and psychological terms. But this would be to exclude much. After all, we ought not to be cynical enough to want to cure all

[17] E. Zamyatin, *Wir* (Cologne–Berlin, 1968), pp. 166 f.
[18] Cf. J. B. Metz, "Reform und Gegenreformation heute", *loc. cit.*; H. R. Schlette, "Der Geist in der Flasche, oder: Sind Orthodoxien möglich?", in *Veränderungen im Christentum* (Theologia publica 12) (Olten–Freiburg, 1969), pp. 11–18.

the tensions within the Church by means of group sociology and psychology. Sociological and psychological laws, rules and behaviour play their part, of course, but what we are dealing with here is a "conflict" of ideas which I believe to be on a different and more serious plane, given the context of the faith, from any other intra-group antagonism. Doubtless it would also be dogmatically incorrect to raise the Church to a supranatural, inapprehensible, meta-historical status for no discernible reason whatever, and thus pull the difficulties and conflicts arising out of partial identification down to the less relevant level of ecclesiastical sociology.

There is nothing, therefore, in dogmatic, moral or pastoral theology, nothing in spirituality or in Church politics, that prevents us from seeing true loyalty and solidarity in certain forms of partial identification. If it is true that partial identification in the sense of a permanently self-critical *sentire cum Ecclesia*—going as far as explicit refusal and protest—is true identification with a Church that can never claim to have a total hold on its own truth, destiny and perfection because it is still "on the way", then a number of consequences follow of which I shall go on to name a few.

Partial identification will express itself in every local community in different forms according to the groupings and interests of these same communities. Parties or factions within the Church cannot be excluded since they are meaningful forms of institutionalizing within the pattern of partial identification— especially not in view of the irreconcilable factions in Corinth (cf. 1 Cor. 1. 10–17).

Partial identification eludes any measured comparison with total identification. Given that it can lead to situations for which individuals alone are accountable (we may think of Camilo Torres or the student community at Amsterdam), the "oneness" of the Church becomes more than ever dependent, in the concrete, on the genuine trust inspired by the all-uniting Petrine office. Thus separation can no longer occur as the result of purely verbal disagreements, but only from refusal of trust—whether on the part of the official authority or on that of the partially identified. From another angle it may be asked whether the highest ecclesiastical office, too, can be thought of as in essence only partly identified—even though it may see itself differently. For by reason of its involvement in its own history and in what is canonically valid in its own time, it can play no part in the legitimate theological experiences and insights of those who are all too hastily and polemically described as partially identified.

If true identification is not total identification (for otherwise the historical existence and dialectic of the Church cannot be understood), then those who—by reason of the higher obedience of partial identification—are attempting to guide the Church into the future with all the aids of modern science and modern thought, are the leaders in our search for new options and a new sensibility. This is so not because it is a matter of safeguarding the Church's *de facto* power and magnitude but because the things of Jesus are at stake, which are mightier than the things of the Church, and cannot simply be equated with the latter though, looked at in the abstract, the two are identical. Finally, there now is great hope of reform in the Church not least because the bishops themselves have become aware of the place of partial identification in their own vocation and rule.

The concept of partial identification makes possible a greater freedom in ecumenical matters, not only because of the distance vis-à-vis *de facto* Catholics, but by reason of inspiration through the Gospel and the things of Jesus, on which true creative partial identification is built.

It is not by direct reference to the texts, but from the analogy between certain Church experiences, and the Church's position as regards the modern process of secularization and emancipation, that we can define the scope of partial identification[19]—in other words by a concentration on the essentials. New bounds are set to the profession of faith. The old tension between Gospel and Church becomes once more visible, mediated through the history of modern times. But in such a fashion that now, the fiction of a totally identified Church having at last been exploded, the followers of Jesus, his disciples (*methetai*) can at last meet each other in a new "oneness".

Thus our thesis that partial identification is true identification brings us once again to the old question of who is a Christian.

[19] Cf. H. R. Schlette, "Die Auswirkung der Säkularisierung auf 'die Kirche' ", in *Aporie und Glaube, loc. cit.*, esp. pp. 342-8.

More important than the question itself, which in its brevity becomes ever more obsolete and irrelevant, is the fact that it is once more being urgently asked, and that concentration upon it can be seen as the welcome result not only of partial identification but of certain theological articulations of it as, for example, the "death of God" theology.[20] In the light of the phenomenon of partial identification present-day theology is less and less inclined to pronounce on who is a Christian, though it would have greater right to do so than an authority working with the concept of total identification, and greater right, too, than certain individuals who make unthinking statements on the subject of a problematical, pre-theological Catholicism.[21] Hans Küng's Brussels formula has already become an important utterance in this field.

Let us once more remind ourselves of the different meanings contained in the concept of partial identification. Our purpose is neither to accept nor to discard the concept *tout court,* but to expound it in all its varieties and to give it its positive and negative character. In the concrete case each man will experience for himself the embarrassment of attempting to place himself between the two poles of a total and a minimal partial identificaton. But despite the unavoidable linguistic and actual subtlety of the distinction as analysed here, the ideas suggested may lead to a clearer and more conclusive understanding of the historical, sociological and pneumatic dynamics of the Church.

This is suggested among other things by the existence of a difficulty which we cannot pursue here, but must at least refer to. In conversation with non-Christians one always finds that they assume total identification to be the norm for Catholics. If one goes on to mention the reality of a critical and creative partial identification, one meets with the astonished counter-question— "But is this attitude fully 'Catholic'?" ... We cannot reproach non-Christians for this view. Who should have given it to them except ourselves, and the "ideas" we have just been speaking of?

[20] Cf. H. Küng, *Menschwerdung Gottes,* Eine Einführung in Hegels theologisches Denken als Prolegomena zu einer künftigen Christologie (Freiburg, 1970), pp. 216–21, esp. 217.

[21] Cf. H. Maier, "Vom Getto der Emanzipation. Kritik der 'demokratisierten' Kirche", in *Hochland* 62 (1970), p. 389, n. 12. Maier's intention here is to pose the question, "Since when do theologians decide who is a Christian?"

In truth there are too many things in the Church, with which one cannot fully identify. Only when the idea of partial identification is no longer suspect but is held up everywhere as the one true form of identification, shall we possess in the eyes of our non-Christian friends the sort of credibility without which true "witness" is not possible.

Translated by Simon and Erika Young

Trutz Rendtorff

Christianity without the Church?

THE tension between "Christianity" and "Church" consists in the manner in which the current debate concerning autonomy, and a self-awareness critical of institutional structures, have achieved theoretical and practical expression in theology and belief. The resultant distinction between Church and Christianity recalls the Enlightenment and provides the permanent framework within which Christian faith is forced to clarify itself in terms of its specific contemporary structure. But by distinction in this case, we should not understand a straightforward, undialectical break between Church and Christianity, but rather the development of the theological framework in which the Enlightenment's emphasis on autonomy finds contemporary expression in man's understanding of the world and of his position in it as a religious creature. It therefore follows that if we are to grasp the positive role of this distinction with regard to the problems that now beset theology, we must appreciate its significance from the viewpoint of fundamental theology. From this point of view, we are considering a distinction different from that other distinction and tension that exists between "Church" and "world", and one that takes priority over it in that its objective is to set our experience of the contemporary world within a homogeneous context of theological understanding of reality.

I. STRUCTURES OF THE DISTINCTION BETWEEN CHURCH AND CHRISTIANITY

The distinction under discussion has a cognitive, religious, political and scientific aspect. The subject should therefore be discussed under these main headings before we turn to their consequences.

(a) Enlightenment theology—in Germany most particularly during the second half of the eighteenth century—developed the distinction between Church and Christianity primarily at the cognitive level. The objective was to establish the truth of the Christian faith in terms that were fresh and universal and therefore in contrast with the formal claims of ecclesiastical tradition. This, then, was a theological outlook that saw the prevailing ecclesiastical understanding of faith as something determined in its essential details by an authority that because it was heteronomous must therefore be in conflict with man as an individual and autonomous being. The distinction between Church and Christianity, therefore, gives voice to a criticism levelled at the merely external, institutional mediation of this truth.

Opposed to the formal claims of tradition was the Christian truth that can only be acquired with the truthfulness of Christian self-understanding. The foundation for this distinction is the insight that the historical mediation of truth must of itself develop into the history of the freedom. As history of freedom, the history of truth is primarily located within man's understanding of himself. This understanding is the source from which all other modes of life and all institutions must drink. A critique undertaken in the interests of freedom therefore directs itself first at all theories of history, and their literary expression, that go against the unity of contemporary self-awareness. And where ecclesiastical doctrine recognizes the human subject only as the addressee and receiver of the Christian truth, the Enlightenment stressed his self-awareness as productive, knowing subject. Tradition is examined from the point of view of the striving for knowledge evident in its form and content.

This in turn means that Christianity is always a part of a growing theological framework, which is itself the measure against which the Church's normative tradition is relativized. In this way, the universality of Christian truth is made possible in the form of a self-supporting body of knowledge which, being something historical, can be traced back to the effort that produced it. The universality of this truth, in the form of the history of the freedom of truth, is pre-eminently and most appropriately located within the Christian self-awareness. The most constructive characteristic of contemporary theology then becomes evident, namely its inability no longer to rest uncritically upon tradition. The distinction between Church and Christianity can thus clarify our understanding of "Church" in terms of contemporary Christianity. This happens where the Church, as the communal striving for knowledge of the Christian self-awareness, that is as a local Church community, is understood as something in process—an understanding now dominant in Protestant theology.

(b) At the cognitive plane, the distinction between Church and Christianity corresponds to the differentiation of theology from religion. As the occupation of theologians, theology is to be seen as a particular type of scholarship, as an accomplishment, which in relation to the general religious experience of reality has its own special character. As universal dimension of experience, religion concerns all men and thus cannot be restricted to the specialized professional knowledge of the theologian. Christianity as religion emancipates; its objective is liberation of life from the pre-structured orientations of particular theological erudition. Something that has nothing in common with religion cannot claim validity as something proper to theology. All special scholarship accessible only to those who have studied theology will ultimately be judged by religion. Theology that has developed in the service of Church and its particular life form must justify itself ultimately in terms of the general life form of religion. The philosophy of religion in its various guises thus reclaims for itself Christian theology's title to universality. Saying what religion actually is then emerges as a new and special task, and one that is not adequately covered by the formulas and resources of ecclesiastical theology.

Contemporary discussion about religion then becomes a medium for the clarification of reality in the light of experience. The institutional identity of religion is not guaranteed exclusively by the Church. In competition with the Church, other life forms such as the family, the nation, the State, the free union of citizens, become further reference points for such supra-individual identification. The distinction between theology and religion tends therefore to prefer the field of ethics as the universal framework of religion. In this context, and pursuant to the distinction between Church and Christianity, the Church is also included. In this spirit the ethical forces within the empirical religious subject are furthered in preference to an emphasis on the Church's own educational function.

The Church is also further involved through the nature of its reform in accordance with the yardstick of the larger ethical identity of Christianity. But the Church is also involved where it is appealed to as the authority for the prevailing moral principles for the conservative understanding of human existence. The extreme ethical sensibility corresponding to the dominant concept of religion leads then also to the experience of change. For the guardians of morality, the Church included, are then inevitably recognized and examined as products of human behavioural activity. They are not independent constants unconnected with the process of life and experience. The yardstick against which the appropriateness or inappropriateness of an institution to life is measured is not permanently fixed but must constantly be determined afresh. To this extent, we can detect a political aspect within the emancipatory understanding of religion as distinct from theology.

(c) In the nineteenth century, the distinction between Church and Christianity was also expressed in political terms. The Church became recognizable as a group of conflicting sects that in relation to Christianity generally looked like religio-political parties. But this is not a situation that can be changed in the first instance at the level of Christianity understood as Church. At this point, a further structural characteristic enters in: the contemporary world tries to develop political dominion and authority out of the productivity of the human urge towards self-determination. Previously, Church and politics were generally accredited with the task of administering the world, a task that in a fundamental sense consisted in restraining the world and its inhabitants within a pre-ordained order. But in our present understanding of things, the urge towards autonomy makes headway through the belief that the construction of the political order is man's primary political task. In this process, the historically defined confessionality and identity of the Christian

Churches gives way to a new political confessionality modelled on the basic characteristics of the political world.

Catholicism and Protestantism—one might say, in this context, tradition and reformation—then assist in the conceptualization of fundamental political conflicts. Characterized predominantly on the one side by dominion and authority, and on the other by freedom and frankness, new alliances come into being in which the historical confessionality of the Churches assumes a functional character. Interest in a general concept of political reality must therefore seek to free itself from the ecclesiastical-institutional aspect of Christianity. This happens in the struggle for the Christian State. In this struggle, the distinction between Church and Christianity establishes itself afresh. If the State as the embodiment of political reality is a function of established authority, then its Christian character is to be found only within its confessional loyalty. This means that by definition the State cannot represent general political reality but can only establish such reality by force. But if, on the other hand, the State is the political objectivization of the contemporary urge towards autonomy, then its Christian character—not tied to any particular confession—is to be sought only in the independent integration of the political fruits of this drive for, and interest in, autonomy.

In so far as the modern State, as a nation State, is itself only a particular version of political reality, the contemporary subjectivity that produces the distinction between Church and Christianity can appeal to the Church against the State in the interests of the generality of political reality, just as it appeals to the State against the confessional character of ecclesiastical Christianity. For this reason, the political dimension of contemporary Christianity becomes the context within which the formulation of theory is pushed out far beyond the original aims of the Enlightenment in respect of the criticism it sought to make of Church and theology.

Not until our own century are we beginning to see how the overcoming of the particularity of the Churches and the formation of a political dimension of world validity correspond with one another. In so far as it is a part of this process to establish the generality of Christian truth, theology can no more rely on the individual Christian's immediate experience of reality that it is able to fulfil its task merely on the strength of its ecclesiastical connections. For this reason, the formulation of theory within the political field exists in close association with the scientific documentation of man's contemporary understanding of himself.

(d) The distinction between Church and Christianity has a further and general structural characteristic in the dimension of scholarship. In Enlightenment theology, the judgment of the historian, as the pursuit of an independent science, was the instrument through which to relativize the claims to authority of Church and tradition. Therein lies the connection between scientific and ecclesiastical theology. We do not need to document the constant quarrel that existed between them. But we do need to know a little more about what it represented. The scientifically pursued study of theology differs from ecclesiastical theology, in the first instance, not so much in method as in the fact that scientific theology concerns itself with religion and Christianity without permitting itself to be influenced by the immediate interests of the Church as Church. This is particularly evident in the discussion as to whether theology should be pursued as the history and science of religion—whether, in effect, the faculties of theology should not become faculties of religious science.

What is it all about? As the most glaringly obvious example, we could take the school of the history of religion at the end of the nineteenth century: scientific theology then distanced itself from the historically received experience of religion, and turned towards fields not obviously connected with religion. This it did in a context and at a time when, in the Christian world, too, man's understanding of Christianity was losing its immediacy and its internal logic. Turning to the world of religions in the sense of the investigation of a world of experience foreign to religion corresponds to a comparable situation in the world of Christianity: the way in which the distinction between Church and Christianity has developed.

Making theology into a true science, which first and foremost is a process of establishing historical inquiry, and a degree of systematization in keeping with it, reached its richest expression in the school of the history of religion. Liberal theology, claiming broad agreement with non-ecclesiastically defined Christianity as a religious ethic and as political theory, worked out in this phase a radical change in its own dealings with experience. The universality of the Christian religion which the distinction between Church and Christianity is supposed to demonstrate is pushed beyond its own historical definition. The immediate, most implicit and obviously accepted agreement with individual, concrete, religious experience now has to be replaced by the scientific formulation of theory.

In terms of the consequential reduction of theology to a science in the twentieth century there results a new task for theory from the viewpoint of the distinction between Church and Christianity. But it is one that changes the whole structure of our questioning. Before we examine what the change involves, we should look briefly at the consequences of the structure so far outlined for the distinction between Church and Christianity.

II. CHURCHLESS CHRISTIANITY?

(a) The most pressing and problematic consequence of the distinction between Church and Christianity is the notion of "unchurch" that it involves. Of course, an absence of ecclesial enthusiasm, demonstrated in its simplest form by poor church attendances, has always been a problem for the Church, particularly for the Protestants. What is new in this discussion of church and unchurch that has been going on now without interruption since 1800, lies in the following: unchurch goes hand in hand with the attitude that one can very well be a good Christian without participating in the Church's life. What is disturbing about this attitude is its expression of a Christian position independent of the life and presence of the Church. For the essence of unchurch is not a godless break with the Church but rather Christian emancipation from the institution.

But it must be asked if the rejection of the ecclesiastical expression of Christianity is made good by other strongly Christian forms of behaviour? This is the tense question that is now being ever more frequently asked. The problem is most severely in evidence in Europe where it exists in connection with the system of large State-supported Churches.

It is worth mentioning in passing that for a country like the

United States of America the distinction between Church and State is a different matter because that country bears the free Church impress carried over by those European immigrants who had broken away from the massive Church complexes of continental Europe. In Europe, and above all in Germany, there is now a widespread movement afoot to found "free associations" that will serve the independent organization of those who are not sympathetic to institutional Christianity but still desire some form of religious and community presence. The significance of these free associations for the structural organization of Christian and community life should not be underestimated.

However, to examine the sociological development of the question of unchurch in the nineteenth century would be matter for a separate study. Seen as whole, it can be said that the distinction between Church and Christianity has not resulted in a simple split. The expression "unchurchness" is appropriate to a type of Christian attitude that, as ordinarily expressed, rejects the restriction that results from identification with the ecclesiastical life style; yet this Christian attitude has no wish to lose sight of the institutional Church as a point of reference for the definition of its own form of life. It can be seen, therefore, that the expressions "church" and "unchurch" do not cover all the actual circumstances of formal Church membership. The problem lies elsewhere. The Church clearly has a particular task with regard to the generation of attitudes, and the offering of guidance, that it itself finds very difficult to define.

Thus a new avenue of exploration is opened up to Church and theology. For it can readily be seen that there is neither an unambiguously churchless Christianity nor an unambiguously functionless Church. But the need clearly does exist for Church and theology to absorb into their own understanding of reality a Christianity not defined in traditional ecclesiastical terms.

(b) We can now see that a further consequence of the distinction between Church and Christianity is a fresh interpretation of "churchliness". Church and theology have been obliged to explore which form of Christian behaviour flows as a matter of necessity from the normative understanding of their identity. The ecclesiastical life attitudes arising from tradition and convention are being increasingly subjected to criticism, including that of ecclesiastical theology. These critics would wish to replace the established life attitudes with others more active—missionary, or whatever. It would be easy to ignore the parallel relationship between the ceaseless discussions concerning Church reform—as vehemently pursued by the so-called "conservatives" as by the so-called "progressives"—and the orientation problems of non-ecclesiastically defined Christianity. One is entitled to say that this discussion is trying to establish in the ecclesiastical context the precise nature of Christianity's life problems. Even in this connection, there is no call to speak of a straightforward break between Church and Christianity; for even the Church as institution sees itself increasingly as charged to bring about the constructive realization of its own identity.

The theoretical connection with contemporary discussions on the subject of autonomy would soon become evident were one to examine closely the debate about the meaning of Church. It would then be seen that what is meant by the expression "churchliness" is not as unequivocally clear as might appear to be the case. The connection can be at least crudely clarified if we now take up the problem at the point at which it has become most explicit in twentieth-century theology.

III. THE DISTINCTION BETWEEN CHURCH AND CHRISTIANITY IN THE FORM OF RADICAL CHRISTOLOGY

It is well known that Karl Barth, in some sharp criticism, challenged the liberal school of theology to admit that theology must see itself explicitly as a matter for the Church. The churchliness of theology, he argued, is the only legitimation of its specifically theological task. Barth's argument has again and again, and not without reason, been seen as a radical counter-movement against liberal theology's distinction between Church and Christianity. But if we consider the conclusion Barth reached in his *Dogmatik*, we can see that there is another possibility. Barth took the autonomy discussion, situated it firmly in the centre of theological concern, and presented it as christology. Christology is the theological version of the contemporary autonomy debate. It is therefore no accident that in overhauling his early dogmatic work

Barth allows for the definition of the churchliness of theology through the "being" of the Church, namely through Jesus Christ himself.

In Barth's case, this leads ultimately to the conclusion that the Church can have no existence of its own: the existence of the Church is exclusively the result of the mission of Jesus Christ, though of course, as things are, this mission is—though it does not have to be—tied to the existence of the Church. The Church is the receiver of a mission that could be withdrawn from it by the giver at any time. The radically christological line of argument leads theology, inwardly refreshed, to a distinction that in every respect accords with the distinction between Church and Christianity.

In this way Barth's theology destroys claims made for itself by the Church, thus leaving it with nothing it does not have from its role within the universal Christian understanding of reality. The "world", understood crudely as that which is not "Church", is the proper area for the development of christology where christology is understood as the theological version of the autonomous self-consciousness.

From this point, one can move on towards a clearer view of Church thought and action in the twentieth century. A primary influence in the *oekumene*, but also in each individual Church, is the awareness that the Church has to make good the gaps in its understanding of reality. Theological causes oblige the Churches to rise above themselves and to absorb into themselves the tension between Church and Christianity. The occasionally dramatic processes in which this is now happening show that there is more at issue than exclusively, or merely, internal Church problems. On the contrary, the Churches and theology have in theoretical and practical terms entered into some of the problems of the contemporary world. Christianity understood as something distinct from the Church, or, in the language of Karl Barth, the being of Jesus Christ, is reflected back by the world itself.

The problems of Christian praxis are ambiguous because they cannot be grasped in the unambiguous terms of churchliness. They therefore require fresh avenues of thought to be explored and themselves need to be worked out in terms of contemporary relevance. In this connection, we also need to be aware of the political dimension of Christian belief, an awareness of the impossibility of achieving any thorough understanding of reality without the assistance of inter-disciplinary studies, and also the fresh definition of that which, in a sense that is both humanly and religiously relevant, can be described as individual experience.

In these terms, the problem of identity poses itself in a new way. If we take the latest development of theology seriously, then it is clear that we shall not be able to determine the identity of Church and theology unless first belief in practical terms achieves a wider spread across the world. The identity of Christianity and theology can only emerge when they join in the process of a universal theoretical and practical grasping of reality. The associations that have linked themselves to the liberal distinction between Church and Christianity belong to the past. But the productive force of the autonomous self-consciousness to which they have given rise has shown itself to be the power that seizes and permeates everything else. Clarification of the structure of the recent history of Christianity serves to make comprehensible the inner necessity and continuity of current problems in a way that enables to ignore false trails.

Translated by Mark Hollebone

Alfonso Alvarez Bolado

Reflections on Ambiguities in the Use of the Word "Church"

AN examination of ambiguities surrounding the use of the word "Church" is bound to be an inquiry into ambiguities within the Church and in its relationship to the outside world in its definitions of the Christian reality. Here one has to ask if the current stress laid on the socio-cultural and socio-political factors of our pluralistic society has had such a profound effect on ecclesial definitions of reality as to make them appear—to the theologian as much as to the sociologist—like mere Christian variations on the secular theme. If this were so, then "Church" and "People of God" would be equivocal titles masking world views and behavioural models so different from one another as to be sometimes completely contradictory. It would be impossible to find a Christian definition of the reality that was specific enough and at the same time managed to sum up a universal view of the *Corpus Christianorum,* or, if one prefers, the flock of Christ.

It would be impossible here to attempt a description of all the ambiguous definitions that give a partial and equivocal view of the People of God. But they can be typified as falling into two overall positions, by means of their corresponding theological (or, if you like, rhetorical) justifications.

There is in fact now, in the universal Church and in the various Christian Churches, a sort of breach between two theological tendencies (some might say two socio-theologies), each supported by a different set of values. Two theologies that justify two definitions of the Christian reality, and so two particular definitions of human reality. We cannot as yet decide whether the pluralism

implicit in these definitions goes beyond what is *Christianly* ad-
missible. But at the moment there is no doubt that this breach is
both manifesting and fomenting a sectarian fragmentation of
the Church that is certainly weakening the sense of identity of
the *Corpus Christianorum*. These theologies are the legitimation
of those definitions of the Christian reality that prevail in what,
for want of better terms, we can call "the conservative Church"
and "the innovative Church".

The two sets of values on which the two theological justifications rest show in two languages (even two approaches to language), and in two patterns of Christian behaviour, the devotees
of which frequently accuse each other of lacking coherence with
the body of belief they are still supposed to profess. By this I mean
that the two theologies present an utterly distinct understanding
of the most basic root words of the Christian faith: God, Christ,
Church. And consequently, an utterly distinct understanding of
what is meant by the Christian presence in the world, such as
the identity and meaning of the People of Christ within the process of social development with its mutability of values and
meanings. (We are talking, let it be said, of theological tendencies at their most extreme, which is what interests us here. Such
an extreme expression is, of course, not to be found in the works
of individual theologians.)

The theological tendency used to justify the "innovative
Church" insists on a critical reformulation of the content of
faith, on the reform of structures, and on the value of "confrontation" as an effective vehicle for the criticism and transformation
needed both inside and outside the Church. This tendency shows
a deeper and more immediate sensitivity towards the meaning and
importance of the processes of human history and social change.
It stresses that these are not simply external data for the "unchanging People of God" to stand aside from and observe, but,
at least potentially, "epiphanic settings" for the historical appearance and concrete will of God, whose revelation is addressed to
all men—to "Everyman" in his socio-cultural variety, which is
itself an intrinsic part of true human identity.

For this reason, and at a time when the very bases of belief are
being called into question, when established models of knowledge and behaviour are being shown to be inadequate, this

theology prefers to insist—in its efforts to maintain the identity of faith—on a creative and tentative form of religious practice rather than on a repetitive orthodoxy or an accommodating neo-orthodoxy. It requires some form of practice, but stresses that these should be communal, the only sort it believes capable of becoming a visible sign of the People of God. Perhaps, at its most extreme, it might be said that this theological school is looking for a model of orthodoxy in which the content of belief would be objectivized and lived in the community before any attempt was made to define it in "the language of 'visions' or ideas". What is believed has to be put into action and offered to all as the social outcome of a transformed human history before a generation intensely critical of all ideology can hear it proclaimed as "good news".

This greater emphasis on the historical and social sides of man's nature explains both this school's particular critical and even agnostic stance in relation to accumulated dogmatic structures and its greater stress on political action. (It also explains the bewilderment the school evokes among a Christian people whose preaching has been quite devoid of elementary anthropological notions such as man's historicity and sociability, who heard only that everything was unchangeable, and that behaviour was above all something that concerned them as individuals.)

From the ecclesiological point of view, this school will not admit the right of the "memory" of the Church to justify its own history as sacred history, as something apart from the other, profane, history. This would be to make of the Church a sect spending its energy on remembrance of its own historical lumber and defence of its own history against social pluralism and its values. Generally speaking, this school is against any form of dualism in the concept of the relationship between the Church and society, since it considers the sole mission of the Church, as part of the universal human community, to be the discernment in faith of man's unique history, of his possibilities for salvation or for sin, in which the Church itself participates. (Leaving any theological assessment aside for the moment, it is worth just picturing the effect this sort of doctrine would have on the bulk of the faithful, used as they are to thinking in terms of *"Extra ecclesiam nulla salus"*.)

Its view of the Church makes it resistant to any understanding of the principle of authority in the Church expressed according to the "hierocratic" model which has served up till now, for the Church as well as for several secular institutions, which are also called into question. The original Christian affirmation that the ecclesial community is, all of it, a prophetic community on which the spirit of Christ has been poured out, demands a relationship between the "flock" and the "pastors" it chooses to watch over it in which the latter have no mandate to take power as the world understands it. If they were to do this, they would at least run the risk of becoming puppets of the established secular powers, thereby compromising the prophetic and critical powers of the People of Christ entrusted to them.

Closely related to this view of authority is the theme of the "free play" of charisms in the Church. The theology of innovation tends to reduce all human and Christian experience in the bosom of the Church to one level, whereas the bureaucratic apparatus of ecclesiastical administration tends to recognize only those models of Christian reality that it has already "classified", and over which it can exercise effective control. The trouble is that most visible forms of established Christian life—including the institutionally charismatic forms—seem to have adopted the models of respectability and prestige valid in Western bourgeois society. A major indication of this *one-dimensional* reduction of Church life can be seen in the weakness of the Church's presence among men who have no recognized status.

Another aspect of the problem is that the schematized organization and life of the Church brings an inevitable lack of understanding of the new secular values arising from historical change. The world is far more polymorphous than it is allowed to be in ecclesiastical schemata. This restrictedness of view in the Church is bound up with the clerical character of those who function as its most relevant members, and, in general, with the authoritarian nature of the present ecclesial institution. The free play of charisms, which is linked with the opening out of the Church towards all genuine secular views, will not become possible without the free play of criticism within the Church. Without this, there is no way of overcoming the "one-dimensional" nature of the Church, with its attendant danger that the Church, which should be the setting for unanimity only in faith, will be surreptitiously changed into a vehicle of uniformity in the service of all sorts of different interests.

In the field of christology, the Chalcedonian confession of the perfect humanity and perfect divinity of Christ has to be interpreted today as a christological—that is, theoretical and practical —approach to the social process. The Christian message is seen as socially "docetic" today if its faith in the perfect humanity of Christ does not imply the revolutionary struggle of the People of Christ in support of all human values and rights. Concretely, this means a constant struggle in defence of the perfectibility of our *humanitas*, in the context of constant effort to create the economic, cultural and political conditions in which man's constant growth towards perfection can be possible. The Church will have to accept the fact that, "expert in human nature" though it claims to be, the mystery of man and his perfectibility will continually surprise it. Otherwise, its confession of the perfect humanity of Christ would appear as a rationalization detrimental to the new and incalculable possibilities of mankind.

In the same way, the divine transcendence of Christ would only be credible if there emerges, through all the intrahuman and purely human processes of the social system, a critical spirit of freedom capable of making us believe that, in Christ and with him, we are "like God". This is what is being asked when the theological tendency we are describing postulates that christological confession should be a christological *construction* of the present and future of mankind. What it does not make quite clear is whether this christological construction should not be preceded by the dark *kenōsis* of the Cross, which would seem to be a necessary condition if there is to be clear distinction between this theological view and the futurological utopias now in vogue.

Turning now to the doctrine of God, this school is in general allergic to a God belonging to any one tradition. It stresses that the God who can command our hearts and destinies today cannot be primarily the "God of our fathers", accessible only through a set of symbols belonging to the past, and through a history that we, the "sons", can hardly see as other than ambiguous, for all that it is called sacred. But its resistance to the "God of

nations" and the "national theisms" that have given slaughter
a theological fervour is even stronger. Perhaps this is one of the
reasons—and not just the epistemological one—for the increase
in "negative" theology in the innovative Church. It looks for a
less nameable God, so that he cannot be called in vain by names
that disqualify others. It silences the traditional names of God
because it looks for a more critical God, faith in whom would
subject all traditions to the searching glare of analysis of the
egoisms that keep them apart from each other. It looks for a
God who can be newly and objectively experienced as the God
of the hope and freedom of the masses. Then at least the collective faith of the community of those who believe in him could
testify of such a God that he feeds the struggle against the *éternel
retour* of badly-made history, not against everlasting evasion.

All these quests incline this theological school firmly in the
direction of looking for God on the horizon of the future. The
opposing school, to which we must now turn our attention,
points out the ambiguities that can arise from the exclusivity of
this theology of the future.

The tendency we have called the theological justification for
the conservative Church has its sensibilities always alert to preserve intact the "traditional" content of faith. But it undoubtedly
tends to identify the integrity of faith with the cultural, ideological and practical expressions and embodiments of it through
which it has taken its historical course to come down to us.
Though it might make some necessary adjustments, this school
tends to take what one might call the "regime of Christendom"
as the best model of social engineering for preserving the fabric
of the faith. This nostalgia can still be heard in phrases like
"defence of the values of the Christian West", as though this
were some latter-day descendant of the Holy Roman Empire.

The theology underlying defence of the conservative Church
is clearly afraid that the "canonical" model of the Church—the
biblical and historical-ecclesiastical model, that is—will be con-
taminated by modern "non-Christian" ideologies and anthro-
pologies. It fears the Christian faith will be taken over and
rapidly liquidated by the neo-liberalism and neo-Modernism of
contemporary culture. And surely no impartial observer could
deny that these fears at least spring from a sociological sense of

smell superior to that of the other school. (At least if one concedes that the overall objective is the retention of a "mass" Christianity, rather than an *"élite"* one of "in group minorities", which this school accuses the other of heading for.)

All these reasons make it obvious that this theological school will insist on the Church—even as a socio-political entity—not losing its consciousness of identity and distinctiveness over against the world, history and social development. It will tend to regard the ecclesiastical privileges won from society over the ages, and definite recognition of the Church by the civil power, as guarantees of the preservation of what might be called its "climate of subsistence and freedom" in the midst of an increasingly functional and rationalized society. Its defenders will even feel that their preservation of this privileged climate of ecclesiastical freedom is a guarantee of social freedom in general at a time when this is continually under attack from the encroachments of the global administration of modern State technocracy. What they do not seem to have asked themselves in this context is whether liberty in general can best be preserved through the maintenance of exceptional zones of privilege of which the Church is the beneficiary, or whether the cause might not be better served by the Church burying itself along with the masses, without privileges, to make common cause with them in their struggle against the menace that threatens them.

The emphasis this school places on the consistency of the historical subsistence of the Church, separate from society, is paralleled by its tendency to accentuate "hierarchical continuity and authority" as the best guarantee of the Church's survival in the pluralistic flux of the modern world.

While it has a keen sociological nose for what has allowed the Catholic Church to maintain its particular consistency within pluralistic modern culture, this school could be said to show a peculiarly blunt sense of historical criticism when it comes to distinguishing between truly original Christian definitions of reality and the cultural borrowings through which they have been expressed and carried on. This is the real reason why it places so much stress on the existence of a "Christian history" over against the "other history". And this would seem to threaten it with a very real danger of becoming a sect, through its efforts at remaining a social monolith while the human process in general goes in the direction of becoming more critical and less inclined to allow traditionally privileged bodies that cannot give a clear critical justification of their own "definitions of reality".

In the realm of christology this school is concerned to define a Christ whose transcendence and uniqueness in history set him apart from all other "promoters and prophets" of humanity. A Christ, then, who is above all the clear and unique Word of God, whose humanity, while certainly real, is *vicarious, "instrumentum coniunctum divinitatis"* in the language of Thomas Aquinas. Because only this sort of Christ, clearly defined as a privileged moment of human history taken on by him, can be capable of exclusively defining faith and of forbidding "being Christian" to change itself into a humanism tinged with Christian values. Only a Christ conceived in this way can continue to be he in whose name alone "we can be saved", outside history with all its ambiguities, and outside the course of human events with all its progress.

Here it must be said that this school would appear to fail to do justice to the universal "Christic element" which biblical tradition finds running through history and whose distinctive characteristics are certainly found incomparably personified in Jesus of Nazareth. By thus isolating Christ from the "Christic element", it runs the risk of interpreting the Christian following of Christ in an over-restricted way, and failing to do justice to other Christlike figures outside biblical culture, particularly those who figure in the next context of modern critical and political culture.

Turning to the doctrine of God, what is sought is above all a "God who is God", affirming this divinity of his in his sovereignty over the world and man and his unconditional antedating of them both. A God who lends himself first and foremost to an attitude of disinterested contemplation and adoration. There is a fear that a theology that concentrates on temporal tasks may —besides thereby inferring their autonomy—easily become a bad "theologizing" of the new myths of humanity. The God who is the "true God" would never be able to lend himself to the equivocation of a suggestive and facile assimilation to the projected achievements of the "future" city of man. By trying to give God plausibility and verisimilitude, the theology that does this in fact dissolves his identity in that of human endeavour.

Even seen as an unconditional and absolute future, then, *God as God* jealously keeps his transcendence, even with respect to any "theology of the future" which would make the realm of eschatology the exclusive horizon of divine epiphany. God as God, then, only shows his unconditional power of reconciling the future of man in the very fact that he once gave himself in innermost truth to men of the past, using his humanity as the humanity of the promise, and only continues talking to us through the works he performed with those men at that time. God as God cannot cease to be the "God of our fathers", because we would otherwise lose all right to call him the God of the future.

So this theological school is opposed to facile contemporary devaluation of the biblical past and Christian history, and strongly presses the case for "remembering the deeds of God" as the source for the "God of hope". This approach cannot, however, escape criticism on the grounds that it strays towards a certain "theological ontologism" which seems to pay scant attention to the empirical-critical and inductive character of contemporary sensitivity. Nor does it seem to take sufficient account of the ability of modern positive science to engage in critical reconstruction, in purely non-theological terms, of religious history in general and biblical history in particular. Above all, it does not seek to ask itself in all honesty whether divine *transcendence* can show itself in the world in any way other than through an "objective mediation" in the history of man. Not to mention whether men today can be seriously interested in the narration of an "objective mediation" that not only took place in the past but is mediated to them in radically mythologized forms. . . . This "objective mediation" would seem to have to be capable of being experienced in a living form today as the mysterious liberating and transforming force in a community that gives back meaning to God as the force behind a new transformation of history that gives history authentically new qualities.

I said at the outset of this sketch that these two broad theological tendencies described here incorporate and justify a much wider plurality of "Christian" definitions of reality. These form a *continuum* going from the legitimate pluralism of faith to aberrant definitions that constitute real latent or manifest heresies, and clandestine apostasies. Neither of the two schools can claim exemption from the danger of "secularism", understood as the reduction of the original data of the Christian faith by profane ideologies, whether progressive or conservative.

Behind the current ambiguity in the differing Christian definitions of reality lies the real nucleus of the conflict: the modern Church's sudden and belated discovery of human historicity and "sociality"—the discovery that being-man-in-the-world involves possessing a political nature both in tune with and capable of transforming history and himself. Neither the practice of belief nor theology has yet sufficiently worked out the implications of this historicity and sociality with any conviction. If an orthodoxy and orthopraxis of a Christian definition of reality capable of taking these new aspects in the unveiling of the human mystery into account are to be worked out, this will require a long and laborious effort, involving the possibility of historical error and of deformation of the *intentio fidei*.

But one thing does seem clear: if one tries to short-cut this route to an authentic orthodoxy and orthopraxis, by substituting what one might, with somewhat bitter humour, call *orthogony*, this will result in the maximum ambiguity. This "orthogony" would result from a decision to make everything as simple and clear-cut as possible as soon as possible; what it would seek would be a certain malleability (or manipulation) of faith. The temptation to identify orthodoxy and orthopraxis with this "orthogony" is very strong for those who form the "directorial" nucleus of the People of God. This directorial nucleus is still made up of bishops and theologians no less than of the bureaucratic officials of the Holy See. These are all men who are liable, in their human weakness, to find it hard to be patient, and this can lead them to lock themselves in conflict, seeking that caricature of true unity represented by "orthogonal" *dirigisme*, instead of opening themselves to the people and the Spirit—who alone is capable of dragging the Church out of its ambiguity. For if the *orthogonal* solution is the final one, it will matter little whether its ethos is conservative or innovative: the People of God will not live in it.

Translated by Paul Burns

Leo Laeyendecker

The Church as a
Cognitive Minority?

Notes on a Qualification

I HAVE been asked to contribute an article on "The Church as a
Cognitive Minority" and to consider what conclusions could be
drawn from this qualification. The editor has at the same time
drawn my attention to the work of Peter Berger, a well-known
sociologist specializing in the field of religion and the Church.
He it is who has used this term "cognitive minority" in several of
his valuable and often quite inspiring publications, with the intention both of describing the churches and of explaining the
present situation in which the churches find themselves. As a
sociologist, he observes and describes without judging. The question is, however, whether what he observes and describes is really
close to reality. If not, it is questionable when non-sociologists—in
this case, theologians and members of the churches—use such
descriptions of the present situation and the theoretical context
within which they are placed as a point of departure on which to
base theological considerations.

We are, of course, bound to welcome any attempt by sociologists and theologians, whose relationships are often rather cool
(the fault is undoubtedly on both sides), to draw closer together.
Theology needs sociology, but only so long as it is really true to
reality as an empirical, scientific study of human society. Not all
sociology is this, however, and the theologian has to be critical in
his attitude, even in the case of an undoubtedly competent
sociologist such as Berger.

It is admittedly not easy to remain critical when assessing

Berger's work, because he writes with exceptional lucidity and has a compelling style. This is unusual among sociologists, but it has certain dangers. In the first place, then, it is necessary to summarize the most outstanding aspects of Berger's ideas and concepts.[1] In the second place, it is important to comment on these, not only in order to modify them and introduce some more subtle shades of meaning into them, but also in order to see the problem in a rather different light.

The Concept "Cognitive Minority"

The framework within which Berger considers religion and the Church is that of "cognitive" sociology. In his opinion, this is the aspect of sociology that is primarily concerned with the social conditions which determine what is regarded as reality with a human group. People create not only material products, but also fairly stable frameworks of activity in processes of institutionalizing their society. Although these come about as the result of people living and acting together, they also become relatively independent as models of action. These objective forms, which exist outside man and have an obligatory character, do not only arise as the result of action—they only continue to exist because people act in accordance with them. People therefore define why they act as they do, in other words, they define the meaning of their own actions. Language is the most fundamental expression of this activity and it is by language that meaning can be communicated and objectivized and that human experience can consequently be regulated meaningfully.

This meaningful regulation of man's experience includes a legitimation—it explains and justifies institutional action. Various levels can be distinguished in this process of legitimation—from simple objectivization in language, via proverbs, sayings, stories and legends and the specialized language of scientific knowledge to all-embracing justifications and world philosophies. The last may or may not be of a religious nature or, as Berger expresses it, they may or may not include a superempirical reference. These legitimating systems imply a specific definition of reality relating

[1] P. L. Berger, *The Sacred Canopy* (New York, 1967); *ibid.*, *A Rumor of Angels* (New York, 1969); *ibid.*, "Zur Soziologie kognitiver Minderheiten", in *Internationaler Dialog* (1969), pp. 127-32.

either to sectors of that reality or else to the total reality itself. We are here only concerned with the all-embracing definitions of reality which, like all such definitions, consist of cognitive and normative elements, ideas about what is and about what ought to be.

The existence of these legitimating systems—in this case, these definitions of reality—is also relatively independent, but it continues only so long as they are firmly rooted in groups and processes. This is what Berger calls the "plausibility" structure—the unquestioning character of these definitions of reality depends, in other words, on the strength of the social structure in which they are rooted. Just as people can only live together, act and communicate with each other by virtue of an objective reality, so too does this objective reality remain a reality only by virtue of people, groups and processes. The building up and maintenance of the social reality and the changes that take place in it depend on a dialectic relationship between people, social structures and legitimating systems.

Cognitive minorities are groups whose definitions of reality differ from those of the majority. This means very little on its own, of course—what is of importance are its consequences. If they are to preserve the credibility or "plausibility" of their definitions of reality, these minorities are bound to organize themselves in closed groups that are isolated from the outside world. Only very strong social links can provide a strong enough basis for the "objectivity" of their definitions of reality and, if they try to adapt these definitions to those of the majority, this is bound to lead to their own identity being undermined and even lost.

Berger is convinced that this qualification can and should be applied to modern Christianity, above all because the Christian definition of reality is no longer accepted without question. As a consequence, the churches are confronted with a dilemma. They can either try to adapt themselves to the definition of reality accepted by the modern world, or else they can resist this, either remain respectable in the cognitive sense or else become a ghetto of extraordinary figures; either continue to count or else be thrust aside as irrelevant. There is no third choice in Berger's opinion and he regrets that so few Christians are willing to become a real cognitive minority. The definitions of reality made by the modern world are accepted all too easily—and Berger is here referring above all to the theologians—and this has led and is continuing to lead to Christianity becoming more and more undermined.

It is obvious that Berger's view provides both an attractive description and an apparently convincing sociological and psychological explanation of the churches in their present situation. There are also many indications that tend to bear out the truth of what he is saying—a very radical tendency in modern theology, for example, which seems entirely to disregard many Christian doctrines which were, in the past, considered to be essential. This tendency has to a very great extent made tradition relative and, although it seems innocuous enough at first sight, it undeniably represents a serious threat to the whole complex of truths about faith. Those theologians who see their task as defenders of the traditional faith have taken fright and have reacted by closing their ranks. They are convinced, as so many religious minorities have been in the past, that they constitute the small flock of the elect called upon to assume responsibility for the defence of the truth. Berger believes that they have a keen sense of what is in fact taking place and that their warnings have been shown to be true.

Clearly, it is very tempting to use Berger's description as a point of departure and a norm for further theological considerations and it should be possible to do this providing it is a correct analysis. His thesis is, however, open to criticism and I should like to review it critically under three main headings.

I. Is the Description adequate?

The concept "definition of reality" is, like several other concepts used by Berger, extremely vague and hardly possible to apply without being defined more precisely. Confining ourselves here to the all-embracing legitimations, it is possible to say that these are open to specification at various levels. They can be expressed in a very general, unspecified way—for example, that there is or is not a higher power, that there is or is not an order in the universe, that man is or is not alone in reality. On the other hand, they can also be expressed in an extremely systematized and rational way in concrete theological or philosophical systems. In between these two extremes, other intermediate forms are possible—one of these being the rather vague knowledge of faith encountered in many Christians.

Another important aspect is the interrelationship between the various definitions of reality—whether they are mutually exclusive, whether they are very strongly or less strongly contrasted with each other or whether it is simply a question of variations of one general pattern. This is, of course, partly dependent on the level of the specification. At the most general level, there is a fundamental contrast—either there is or there is not a superempirical reality. At lower levels, there is always a question of common denominators—the different specifications have, in this case, the character more of variations than of contrasts. These more precise definitions are important if we are to speak in exact terms about cognitive minorities.

What can be said about the situation itself? As far as the general definition of reality is concerned, it is very much a question of whether those who acknowledge a superempirical reality form a (cognitive) minority. This is the problem of secularization.[2] If this process is described as the "loss of social significance of the (Christian) definition of superempirical reality", it is very questionable whether this process is as far advanced as it is generally regarded as being. The extent to which personal and social life is defined in superempirical terms differs very widely.

Various investigations have shown that very many quite strong convictions about a superempirical reality prevail in the private sphere. This applies particularly to basically human questions concerning suffering and death and their meaning, but is not exclusively restricted to these questions. It is far less true of the public sphere—God plays a less important part in man's economic, social and political activities. The rhetorics that are said to be habitual in religion make little difference to this division between the private and the public sphere, which is regrettable, but apparently cannot be greatly changed. In this context, it is also important to mention the current interest in various forms of mysticism, including Eastern thought, which is connected with the growing conviction that some of man's faculties, such as his

[2] L. Laeyendecker, "A Sociological Approach to Secularization", *Concilium* 7 (Sept. 1969), pp. 6–10 (American Edn., Vol. 47).

sense of mystery, may have become atrophied with the rise of Western rationalism.

This way of speaking about a minority, then, has clearly to be corrected in so far as it is concerned with these very general and less specific definitions of reality. What is more, it has nothing to say about the future. The private sphere may be the last bastion which gives the impression of strength and where it is still possible to detect some sign of life, yet it has undeniably been subject to assault. Predictions about a definitive demolition cannot, however, be based on empirical data—we cannot foresee what kind of answer will be given to questions about the meaning of suffering and death in the future.

It would certainly be very premature to say that any of those answers would be purely secular. What is more, it cannot simply be assumed that the questions themselves can be reduced to the purely individual level—they clearly have a social dimension.

We must also look elsewhere if we are to judge whether or not the term "cognitive minority" is used correctly—in more specific definitions of reality, various theologies, confessions of faith and even in rather vague expressions of belief. The term "minority" would seem to be justified in many such cases, but it is necessary to add a few notes and comments even here.

There are many variations within the one Christianity, from strict orthodoxy, via very many intermediate forms, to extreme liberalism. Compared with all the rest, each one of these variations is a minority, but they all have a very great deal in common and this is all the more obvious the further one moves away from the two extremities. There is, in other words, a pluriformity within Christianity and we may well ask whether Berger's dilemma applies so fully here.

The strictly orthodox variations are probably becoming more and more of a minority, but what does this really mean? According to Berger, a dilemma is implied when we use the term "cognitive minority"—a choice between adaptation and being undermined, or isolation and preservation. It is, however, not entirely clear where the process of adaptation ends and the undermining process begins. What we are ultimately concerned with here is the problem of the extent of change that is compatible with a preservation of identity. As long as it is not clear what it is that determines the identity of Christianity, we may continue to doubt whether the qualification "cognitive minority" is really useful.

There is, in fact, no complete clarity about this. There has always been a certain tension between the concrete, institutional forms in which Christianity—its doctrine, worship, ethics and organization—is expressed and the constantly changing environment. There have always been adaptations—or rather, changes—affecting these forms of expression and these have always been accompanied by discussions about the limits which have had to be observed. In many cases, it has only been by changing that Christianity has been preserved. (There are also many examples of uncritical adaptation—it has, however, seldom been possible to ascertain in advance which forms were right and which were wrong.)

To be completely consistent, however, we ought to apply the term as well to minorities which are not purely defensive, but which are vigorously working towards a renewal of life in the churches. In this case, quite a different light is thrown on the dilemma. In other words, the term "cognitive minority" can only be used meaningfully once the problem of identity has been solved. This is a particularly difficult problem and it is even more difficult to solve it if it is considered principally at the cognitive level. This brings us to our second note on the qualification "cognitive minority".

II. Is it permissible to emphasize the Cognitive Aspects?

There have been many references to the strong emphasis given to the cognitive aspect in the history of Christianity.[3] Theologians have always been engaged in thinking about the attitudes that they should have towards changes and in trying to come to terms with them. Above all, attempts have been made to preserve the true Christian teaching. The practical consequences of this have almost always been regarded as secondary in comparison with the need to continue to proclaim the true faith. There is, however, a remarkable contrast between the importance accorded by the

[3] A. Mirgeler, *Rückblick auf das abendländische Christentum* (Mainz, 1961).

official Church to the true Christian teaching and the part played by the cognitive aspects in Christian life on the one hand and in the criticism of Christianity on the other.

Let us first consider this last point—criticism of religion in general and of Christianity in particular is nowadays directed in the main towards its practical consequences and effects. An obvious example of this criticism is that of Karl Marx. "The social principles of Christianity preach the need for a ruling class and an oppressed class, displace justice to heaven and thus justify the continuation of injustice on earth, explain the base behaviour of the oppressors towards the oppressed either as a justified punishment for original sin or other sins or as tests to which the Lord, in his infinite wisdom, exposes the redeemed, and preach cowardliness, self-contempt, humility and subjection...."[4] Marx also says "the end of religion as the illusory happiness of the people promotes the real happiness of the people. The demand to put an end to illusions about the real situation of the people is at the same time a demand to put an end to a situation which requires illusions."[5]

This is not a direct criticism of the cognitive aspects as such, but of the social consequences of them. It is not a direct criticism of Christian faith as such, but of Christian behaviour. As soon as Christians concern themselves more with the task of opposing social injustice and of promoting the welfare of their fellow men, Marxist criticism becomes perceptibly less. There may even be an increased consciousness on the part of Marxists for the transcendent aspect, which re-emerges as a problem in the attempt to achieve a more humane society.

As far as Christian life is concerned, it would be impossible to deny that ideas have a decisive influence on human action and behaviour—one has, for example, only to think of the extent to which Calvinistic thought influenced the development of capitalism.[6] Equally important, however, is the influence of action on

[4] K. Marx, F. Engels, *Über Religion* (Berlin, 1958), p. 65.
[5] K. Marx, F. Engels, *op. cit.*, pp. 30 f.
[6] M. Weber has written in greater detail about this problem. See his *Gesammelte Aufsätze zur Religionssoziologie*, I (Die protestantische Ethik und der Geist des Kapitalismus) (Tübingen, ⁴1947); *Wirtschaft und Gesellschaft*, I (Cologne and Berlin, 1964), especially pp. 368–404.

the spread of ideas. These very Calvinistic ideas gained ground precisely because they were so relevant to the activity of those who adhered to them. It would be instructive to investigate in some detail the consequences of the less all-embracing differences in Christian teaching for social action (especially within the Church). It is probable that they have, generally speaking, not been very influential. The level of specification is clearly important here too. These consequences might, of course, be regarded—perhaps correctly—as hair-splitting within the Church and therefore as valueless or almost valueless when applied to the problems of man and society.

This indirectly confirms the priority of action—something that is explicitly recognized in many of the formulations made of the problem, which has been given the name of "Church outside the Church". Wherever a genuine attempt to create a more humane society is encountered, there is, in the opinion of many who have studied this question, a Church existing outside the Church and this has little to do with adherence to the teachings of the official Church.

What is the attitude of those who belong to these various existential forms towards the Church, or churches, as communities with an explicit confession of faith? We may say with certainty that the cognitive aspect is clearly secondary here. Finally, it is hardly necessary to point out that political theology is another manifestation of this emphasis on Christian action and on the practical, social consequences of theological thought.

What, then, is really implied by this? In the first place, the value of the qualification "cognitive minority" is made even more questionable. In the second place, the dividing lines are displaced. In Christianity, it is not simply a question and not even primarily a question of those who are faithful to the same teachings, but of those who are impelled by the same ideals of humanity, peace, justice and solidarity. Teachings are clearly of secondary importance.

This does not solve the problem of identity, but it does show in which direction a solution should be sought. The truth must be done and brought to light. If it is not done, there is an undermining and even a loss of identity. This brings us to our third point.

III. A Different Dilemma

To begin with, let me briefly summarize my argument. The concept "minority" has to be relativized if it is to be applied to the least specified definitions of reality. There are undoubtedly minorities at more specified levels, but the concept "cognitive minority" is of doubtful value even here. On the one hand, we have a pluriform situation, which does not necessarily include the dilemma referred to by Berger, and, on the other, this dilemma presupposes an answer to a more fundamental problem, that of the relationship between change and identity. What is more, it is very questionable whether the problem of identity can really be solved at the cognitive level—it is far more a question of activity. Despite this relativization, however, there is still a dilemma, but it is a different one from that referred to by Berger.

The dilemma of adaptation or isolation is not a new one. It can be dated back to the time when Christianity became a State religion under Constantine. Adaptation to the political structures of the empire did not leave the cognitive aspects completely untouched, but it did not confront the leaders of the Church with really serious cognitive problems of identity.

The problems were situated then and are situated now at the practical level—at the level of adaptation to unjust structures. This adaptation was regarded as necessary in order to preserve an influence in society. Any other way, it was argued, would have led to isolation, loss of freedom and conflict. This may well be so, but an attitude such as this did not have to be completely fruitless just because of this.

This dilemma is not to be found, as Berger has contested, at the cognitive level, but rather exists at the ethical level. To express it in its simplest form, those who are concerned about cognitive adaptation are not aware of many difficulties with regard to ethical adaptation. On the other hand, those who regard ethical adaptation as inadmissible are probably inclined to think of the cognitive problems as less important.

What must prevail in this case? This is connected with basic views of the Gospel and the Church. If the second point of view is taken, an answer has to be found to the problem as to how ethical minorities can become really effective, that is, how they can avoid conforming on the one hand and isolating themselves on the other. Both inside and outside the Church, this problem confronts countless movements for (ethical) renewal and so far no really satisfactory answer has been found.

Translated by David Smith

Joseph Arntz

Is there a New Openness to the Church's Charismatic Testimony?

THE traditional charismatic testimony of the Church is expressed in the three vows of obedience, chastity and poverty and institutionalized in the monastic life in the broadest sense of the word. This way of life is at present undergoing a crisis. On the other hand, young people especially are becoming increasingly concerned with the fate of the poor in the world and are voluntarily embracing poverty themselves. Does this perhaps provide the Church's traditional charismatic testimony with a new perspective?

The answer that is usually given is that there is a purely superficial connection between the traditional charisma and those who demonstrate their aversion to capitalist society and that the testimony as such is irrelevant to those whose aim is to improve the fate of the poor.

This rather negative answer implies that what may be a charisma at one period is not necessarily so at another time. I shall discuss this question in the first section of this article and the two parts of the distinction that has been made above in the second and third sections. I can only indirectly touch on the much more basic problem as to how modern man can be made more sensitive to our speaking about God. Finally, I must emphasize, to avoid all misunderstanding, that the essential meaning of the monastic vows is by no means exhausted when one has considered their value as signs.

I

If the apostolic "gift of tongues" were to be bestowed, for example, on the Dutch Church today, the reaction would not be thankfulness but panic. It would not be regarded as a charisma by the believer or as a sign by the unbeliever. The community at Corinth thought of it as a charisma, but the Church as a whole did not think that such events would be repeated again and again and valued positively.

It is apparently not possible to apply this to the evangelical counsels of obedience, chastity and poverty, because they are very deeply rooted in the tradition of the Church and it is only by a special grace of God that they can, according to the gospels themselves, be followed: "If you would be perfect..." (Matt. 19. 21), etc. If, then, they are charismatic gifts, we may hope that God will continue to bestow this special grace on his Church.

On the other hand, however, the evangelical counsels are also extremely subject to historical conditions. Let us first briefly consider poverty. Jesus' counsel to the rich young man was something that was strictly relevant to the economic and religious attitudes of his own period. The poor man was helped economically by alms, but he was also regarded as someone who could expect justice only from God and who had therefore to place all his trust in him, with the result that there was, at that time, a strong religious desire to share in the collective trust that the poor had in God. As soon as man ceased to interpret poverty in a religious sense—and it is only relatively recently that he has finally come to recognize poverty as a structural phenomenon—then, for a very long time, he did not know how to deal with the problem. The name "poverty" was retained in monastic communities, but it was experienced as sobriety and obedience—the member of the community was only allowed possessions with his superior's permission.

What about chastity? In a recent plea for celibacy, it has been suggested that the words of the gospel—making oneself un-marriageable "for the sake of the kingdom of heaven" (Matt. 19. 12)—should be interpreted against the background of the problem of divorce in the preceding verses. The author, however, observes "that their meaning need not be limited to this, because the experience of the Church is not limited to the text of Scripture".[1] One would agree formally with this statement, but the whole social context of the Church—in which dualism has always played such a great part—is reflected in her experience and this surely has led to a selective reading of scriptural texts.

The ways in which monastic obedience has become institutionalized are also a faithful reflection of the ways in which the various communities have been conditioned historically by the societies in which they first originated. The concept of the Augustinian superior "whom thou must obey as a father"[2] and of the father abbot of the Benedictine order goes back to the idea of the paterfamilias in later antiquity. The mendicant friars of the thirteenth century are examples of an emerging democracy. The Jesuit spirit reflects accurately the sixteenth-century impulse to conquer and to plan, put at the service of the kingdom of God, and there was a need for absolute obedience if this were to be achieved. Both impulses were aspects of emergent capitalism.

The part played by Peter Lombard's *Sententiae* in the history of theology is well enough known. One of the results of this type of writing was that passages of Scripture and of the Church Fathers which had become dissociated from their literary and historical context began to lead an independent life of their own. At the time of the *Summae*, various statements were fitted into a great systematic whole, among them those about the three vows—poverty (external goods), chastity (goods of the body) and obedience (goods of the soul). This, it should be noted, was fully in accordance with a scheme which, though customary at the time, was much earlier in origin.

If we examine how this scheme was used, in Thomas's *Summa*, for example,[3] then the underlying presuppositions are clearly revealed. Medieval man thought that there was an order, a hierarchy of "goods", at the summit of which was God, the highest good. The man who wished to love God more than anything else therefore chose to love him more than money, sexual pleasure

---

[1] A. Durand, "Recherches sur le sens de la vie religieuse", in *Lumière et Vie*, 96 (1970), pp. 54–90; also published as "Peiling naar de zin van het religieuze leven", in *Tijdschrift voor Theologie*, 10 (1970), p. 238.

[2] Rule of St Augustine, Ep. 211.

[3] Thomas Aquinas, *Summa Theol.*, I–II, q. 2, o.

and freedom. This teaching was completely in accordance with the medieval view of the world as a teleologically ordered whole surmounted by the one highest good. The monastic vows were consequently given an important place in this ordered system, within which all those who shared the underlying presuppositions had to give their consent to the monastic vows.

This intellectual consent was, however, not the same as the attitude of the man who suddenly felt that he was personally addressed by a passage in Scripture—as Augustine and Francis were—or as that of the man who was powerfully influenced by a saintly or persuasive religious figure who embodied that biblical teaching in his life. Encounter with such a figure would lead to a perception of a whole structure and a value judgment of that whole, which, if analysed, would make what we say seem an objective judgment even though it is essentially a value judgment. If we allow this whole to be broken down into different qualities, the scale of values of those qualities will reflect us too as children of our time.

Let me illustrate this with a concrete example. We in the twentieth century are conscious that the Curé d'Ars imitated Christ more in his great patience than in his eating habits. Medieval man, on the other hand, was very conscious of mortification. A sign for one generation is not necessarily a sign for other generations.

There is, however, more at stake here than simply a question of changing tastes. We have to consider seriously whether or not the whole structure of vows is connected with a view of the world, of man and of God which modern man can hardly accept. Is the underlying presupposition of this medieval attitude perhaps not that of the man who is led, "by the absence that he experiences in himself",[4] to look for what is meant by the word "God" in religious thought, but who then pulls the transcendental reality down to his own level and tries to keep hold of it by calling it the "highest good"?

II

Modern man, I think, prefers to look in a different direction.

[4] *Ibid.*, II–II, 85, 1.

Bonhoeffer once said that God is among us in our lives and not on any side.[5] He is no longer thought of as the one who fills in all the gaps in our lives, but as the culmination of the fullness of human existence.

Catholic theology has also followed a similar course during this century. Christian humanism led to the idea of an "incarnational" Christianity, which has in turn been followed by a dialogue between Christians and Marxists. This interchange of ideas has made some Christians at least aware of the danger of letting an assessment of human values remain purely at the level of talk and of the need to oppose in action the social structures that hinder the development of those values. Finally, it has become increasingly clear that any theology of secular realities had eventually to become a "political" theology.

This "political" theology has been developed at a period when many young people have chosen to go their own way—a way that is more left than that of neo-capitalism and more right than that of bureaucratic and rigid communism. Their opposition takes many forms. Vastly simplifying a complex situation, we may say that the "hippies" are more opposed to the spirit of middle-class society, whereas the young revolutionaries are opposed not only to its spirit but also to its structures. The "hippies" or neo-mystics[6] live in voluntary poverty and practise contemplation and ritual. The revolutionaries are actively concerned with the fate of the poor and oppressed in Western society and in the underdeveloped countries. Is there a new openness among these young people to the Church's traditional charismatic testimony? Dare we hope for this?

Above all, both the "hippies" and the young revolutionaries regard the Church as part of the establishment that they oppose so strenuously. Firstly, they cannot accept her teaching about sex, which is admittedly influenced by nineteenth-century attitudes. Secondly, they dislike her apparent acceptance of capitalist ethics, and thirdly her wealth and silence about the existing economic and political order. Fourthly, they reject her centralized

[5] D. Bonhoeffer, *Widerstand und Ergebung* (Berlin, 1961), p. 147; English trans., *Letters and Papers from Prison* (London, ³1967).
[6] Harvey Cox, *Feast of Fools* (Cambridge, Mass., 1969).

and authoritarian structure and her restriction of her members' freedom.

The "hippies" travel great distances to escape from the society on which they still live, by begging. They are, as it were, the negative of the positive picture of post-Renaissance Western society, with its urge to work, to produce and to acquire and its emphasis on calculating, rational thought. They value being more than having and uncalculating self-expression more than rational thought. They sing, dance and sit in the sun, behaving like the ancient cynics in the twentieth century. They celebrate life in aimless, useless activities which are an end in themselves and a pure expression of being. They are therefore direct and unconventional in their relationships. War is seen as a disposition ("make love, not war"). Their attitude to sex is pre-conventional, because their return to a direct experience of life means a return to the body as the point of entry into the world. The same applies to their use of drugs. Descriptions of "trips"[7] gives the impression that they have a need to make themselves and the world less real and to return to the pre-personal and pre-voluntary subjective level which forms the basis of man's necessarily limited conscious life.

It is all too clear that we cannot expect the traditional charisma of the Church or the three monastic vows to make any appeal to these young people. Their community is, moreover, based on chance meeting and is not lasting. All the same, they have a valuable contribution to make. As the heirs of puritanism, we have lost all sense of celebration and know nothing of the spirit of Francis's hymn to the sun. The "hippies", on the other hand, affirm life powerfully and, in so doing, perhaps provide a key for modern man to understand what is meant by the statement, made in faith, that God exists and is good.

III

The revolutionaries regard the existing order as alienating and want to change it as quickly as possible. Like the "hippies", they feel that it is no longer possible to *be* and to be creative, but they also protest against the established order because of the poverty

[7] Timothy Leary, *The Politics of Ecstasy* (London, 1970).

and exploitation that it causes and tolerates. They are on the side of the poor, the persecuted and the underprivileged. They affirm humanity and feel angry and frustrated because the Church seems to be in league with the established structures and does not protest against injustice or seem to be, despite her claims, a Church of the poor.

This desire for spectacular achievements—which is often a deceptive way of acquiring a good conscience—may make us fail to see the unspectacular field work that is being done everywhere all the time. This should be a sign not only to us, but also to those for whom it is done. Earlier in this article, I mentioned the sobriety of monastic poverty and I may add here that it is this collective sobriety which enables so much unspectacular field work to be carried out.

Those whose aim is to change the structure of society inevitably feel that this field work is unimportant. But the poorest of the poor are never revolutionary. Their level of aspiration is always low and their frame of reference is confined to their immediate surroundings. They may perhaps benefit from a revolution, but can never bring one about. The low level of aspiration in the poor is connected with the character of poverty itself. The really poor man is too poor to free himself from poverty, which he and the generations that follow him regard with a certain fatality.

The man who voluntarily shares the life of the poor therefore acts as a piece of the leaven of freedom in the lives of the poor. Because he chooses his poverty, it does not contain that note of fatality. By putting himself, as a more educated person, at the service of the poor, he introduces freedom. He can draw attention to breaches of the law, express grievances and find his way for the poor through the bureaucratic maze. A slight improvement may lead to a loss of that sense of fatality among the poor and reveal possibilities which had hitherto been concealed. The man who voluntarily embraces poverty can therefore be a sign giving hope.

To accept that the established structures of society must be changed is to imply that they can be changed. It is sometimes said that theocracy breaks through ontocracy. The man who believes in God cannot regard any structure as unchangeable and unconditional, so that faith in God should entail a great openness to the future. (This is, of course, very difficult for those who think that some structures are subject to the natural law or the order of creation and who regard that law as an expression of God's will to accept.) The real difficulty, however, is that our conviction about the contingency of all structures is no longer a theologoumenon—we no longer believe in it, but know it. That is why it is very difficult to be aware of a really striking testimony of the passage "For the form of this world is passing away" (1 Cor. 7. 31) in the monastic vows and especially that of chastity.

If the structures of society can be changed and there is a strong desire to change them, we at once enter the sphere of what may be called the effectiveness of aims, which is quite different from that of the relationship between the sign and its significance.

The first question to be asked in this sphere is whether the monastic vows make it easier for the man who takes them effectively to achieve this aim. We may hope that men are more committed and ready to take greater risks on the basis of those vows, and this is often the case, but it does not always happen. More married Protestant ministers died in the resistance during the Second World War in the Netherlands than celibate priests, but this, of course, takes us away from theology into the sphere of statistics. It is not certain whether Catholic priests are more intensively concerned with the work in their parishes than their married Protestant colleagues.

Finally, a word must be said about the aim that it is hoped to achieve by changing these structures. Ultimately, it is a question of achieving more justice for more people. Christians are in the habit of seeing this in the light of the eschaton, but this is above all an interpretation made in faith of the present together with everything that this present contains in the way of achievements (in the past) and dynamism (in the future). Every partial realization of justice is an attempt, brought about by an inner dynamism, to increase justice. Every partial affirmation of justice contains an affirmation of absolute justice. What we must tell non-believers, then, is that this is precisely what believers mean when they say that there is a God—that he exists and that he is good.

Translated by David Smith

Karl Rahner

Orthodoxy and Freedom
in Theology

NOTE: The letter reprinted here is not an intellectual exercise. It was written for a specific reason. A number of deletions have been made to prevent the individual case with which the letter is concerned from being recognized. The problem under discussion is still clear in spite of the deletions, and the case has in any case now been shelved since the objections to Mr NN's ideas have been retracted and he is now able to continue teaching. Attempts by readers to discover the person concerned at the time this letter was written would therefore be superfluous.

Dear...,
I am writing to explain my position on the objections which have been brought to my notice and make it necessary to determine whether Mr NN is a suitable person to continue teaching in the Theological Faculty of your University.

I. PRELIMINARY NOTES

1. I shall confine my remarks to the copy of the lecture which has given rise to certain complaints. I have had an opportunity to read a second manuscript on similar problems but I do not intend to refer specifically to the latter text because I feel that it would not alter my judgment and also because the objections made by a higher authority refer only to the first lecture.

2. I realize that a detailed analysis of my position in this matter would require a much fuller presentation and interpretation of Mr NN's doctrine than I am able to provide here. If a theologian

presents his theological concepts in a new, indeed creative and original, manner and if he does so by his own admission hesitantly and questioningly in the context of a theology which is still searching for its own *raison d'être*, the understanding, presentation and interpretation of his doctrine cannot be dealt with in a few pages. But I simply do not have enough time and energy for such a critical analysis. I must therefore ask you to accept this short contribution and allow me, in this instance too, the theological credit which you have granted me on other occasions.

3. I must immediately put on record my strongest protest against the report by one of Mr NN's colleagues which you attached to your request for my opinion. I am quite unable to accept that report, which makes not the slightest effort to consider Mr NN's work in its totality and fails to examine its central ideas or ultimate objectives. A number of suspicions are merely expressed in the space of half a page without any attempt to support the assertions made by quotations and page references. When, for example, has Mr NN. clearly stated that he rejects the inspiration of the Scriptures? On what concept of inspiration does his opponent base this judgment? Is his notion of inspiration binding on every Catholic theologian? All these questions are evaded with the words "... cannot be understood otherwise than as. . .". Does the Gospel according to St Mark speak of the "divinity of Christ" in the same way as the Gospel according to St Paul or John? Should a modern theologian not draw the attention of his audience to the clearly perceptible development of Christology in the NT? If Mr NN suggests that Jesus believed in the *parousia* as imminent is he not in accord with respected modern Catholic exegetes? Can this problem simply be overlooked—as previous Catholics overlooked it—without appearing dishonest and ineffectual or incredible in the eyes of the audience? What is the meaning of the complaint (vague again: "it seems to us . . .") that Mr NN presents a "situation-oriented dogmatics"? If this suggests that the NT theology is conditioned in some measure by contemporary horizons of understanding, the statement is merely a platitude which is obvious to any exegete and dogmatist. The problem with which Mr NN is also concerned only begins at this point: i.e., the question which is the basis of all hermeneutics, as to how, under historically conditioned and therefore changing

horizons of understanding, the same reality can be designated and expressed differently under different horizons of understanding and how these statements can be compared and the ultimate identity of meaning ascertained. In my opinion, the report in question completely ignores these problems. If Mr NN feels that traditional concepts such as "sacrifice" and "atonement" contain certain ideological elements which have lost their relevance, this should surely not make his ideas suspect from the outset without any more precise evidence.

The whole history of Catholic theology with its widely varying theories of sacrifice and redemption shows how efforts to "de-mythologize" and "deideologize" have always been at work, even if this cannot be demonstrated by individual examples. If Mr NN and his modern audience react more sensitively on such matters than the author of this report (and perhaps than many formulations in the NT), and if he seeks to eliminate modern difficulties of understanding and faith by hermeneutics as such and not simply by subsequent definition of certain concepts (such as the "anger" of God, or "blood" which redeems and sanctifies, etc)., in my opinion his arguments cannot be dismissed *a priori* as errors or heterodoxy. No proof has been evinced as to why he should necessarily refer to the theology of sacrifice in the OT. (I shall examine the use of Protestant theology in another context.) I have now answered all the points made in this dubious half-page report. I am amazed and horrified by the procedure followed in this report which concerns the life of a human being and theologian whose theology has a right to be taken seriously and whose scholarly and scientific freedom must be respected. This method of dismissing a theology is even worse than the procedures adopted in the days before the Council. If such methods became public serious damage would be done to the Church, which would be accused once again of proceeding with totalitarian methods and without regard to men and their rights, against any ideas which do not fit neatly into place in the "system" and conventional hackneyed models.

II. On the Problem of Didactics in Theology

1. A number of general considerations must be taken into

account before examining Mr NN's teaching methods in terms of didactic ability (to the extent that the latter is revealed in the copy of the lecture). Today teaching must be given in German. This necessarily entails changes in the previous traditional method of teaching scholastic theology according to which tuition and lectures were given in scholarly Latin. In addition, an honest and sober study shows that the decree *Optatam totius* of the Second Vatican Council (No. 16) stipulates a completely different teaching method for dogmatic theology than was normal in traditional scholastic theology. The latter was strictly analytical and started out from a ready-made thesis which had to be proved; concepts were analysed and arguments adduced from the different *loci theologici* for the given thesis.

The new method proceeds by synthesis: first the biblical themes must be specified and then supporting evidence must be brought from the history of theology which extends on the one hand into the general history of the Church and spiritual history (this is the intention, although in fact such procedures have so far not been adopted in our scholastic endeavours), and on the other hand is supposed to lead closer to St Thomas; at the same time, this treatment of theological doctrines must be brought into contact with the human problems of our own age. When we consider this silent revolution undertaken by the Council (which certainly does not seem beyond dispute to me but nevertheless has the authority of the Council behind it), we are bound to tread carefully in objecting that Mr NN has adopted a method of teaching which is not suitable for the clear and firm training of theologians. But anyone who follows the method of the Council runs the risk of exposing himself to the same objection.

2. The professor of theological dogmatics is in a very difficult position today. From the standpoint of modern exegesis (which he must represent), of modern philosophy (which no longer recognizes any homogeneous form of neo-scholastics which would be readily acceptable), of the enormous variety in the history of dogma, of contact with Evangelical theology (which is the duty of the modern dogmatic theologian), the problems of his discipline have become almost inconceivably more complex and difficult than they were only thirty years ago, and still seem to our elders, who have simply not become aware of the new situation. How is

a professor to be true to the situation and challenge of his science today? What is he to do when he is faced with unsolved problems which he honestly—and not in mere words—recognizes as such; with problems which have not been solved but affect the very substance, the meaning and existence of the truth of the faith? If he tries to hide the difficulty of the present situation from his pupils because they are not yet mature enough to grasp it and would be faced with an excessively difficult problem, he will find that one group among his students realize that he is evading the issue and question his credibility, while a second group will still be satisfied because of their lesser ability or traditional physical and mental background—but they too will find later on that they have not been adequately prepared for the spiritual climate in which they will one day have to live.

If the professor adopts the opposite approach and introduces them as far as possible to his modern knowledge of the science with which he is concerned, many of his students will—at least to begin with—feel overstretched, until they slowly become acclimatized to the new spiritual environment in which we live— although perhaps not *every* professor likes to accept the reality of modern life. It is indeed perfectly conceivable that this justified (if not inevitable) method of teaching may unfortunately coincide with a crisis in the life of the student—a factor which is impossible to predict—and bring about a crisis of faith which may lead to a catastrophe—but the catastrophe is the responsibility of the student and his environment and not of the professor.

These are very abstract considerations which cannot be illustrated here by concrete examples. But to realize the true implications of this situation we must remember that almost all the exegetical and biblical theological decisions taken by Rome between 1900 and 1950 and accepted without question or even energetically defended only ten years ago have now become obsolete, and can no longer honestly be defended by a dogmatic theologian today—unless he believes he is a better exegete than the bulk of Catholic exegetes teaching today who reject those decisions of the Vatican without exposing themselves to criticism from dogmatic authority (cf. my essay in the February 1970 issue of *Stimmen der Zeit*).

A similar criticism could also be made of many positions which used to be sacrosanct in neo-scholastic philosophy and were taken as the basis of theology. Even twenty or thirty years ago, neo-scholastic theology was perhaps well acquainted with the history of dogma and theology (e.g., Ehrle, Grabmann, Landgraf), but this knowledge did not rub off on the scholastic school theories of these dogmatists. All we need to prove this is to compare one of the school dogmatic systems which were current until recently with the old Wirceburgensian systems. Today the old assumptions simply do not hold good. Serious study of the history of dogma and theology makes a much more cautious, looser interpretation of dogmatic theories necessary and shows that—without impairing the substance of the faith—meaning can be expressed in widely varying ways, so that it may be difficult for the observer to recognize the same idea in a new form. The teacher of dogma in this modern context must adopt a very *catholic* attitude if he is to do his duty. He is bound to experiment. He must make a more or less random selection from an almost boundless sea of material and problems. Whether he likes it or not, he no longer has the backing of a truly homogeneous school theology which he could simply hand down and defend. In modern pluralist theology (see my essay on this subject in Volume 9 of my *Theological Investigations*) there can be no uniform "canonical" method of teaching dogma.

3. Having regard to these facts, I believe that the strong objections made in public against Mr NN's teaching method with a view to demonstrating his unsuitability to occupy a professorial chair, are unjustifiable. I do not deny the fact that his method approaches the limits of the demands which one can make today on a young student of average ability. Because I am aware of the advantages of the previous analytical teaching method, in which the student was given a limited but intensive quantity of school knowledge, I can see clearly the drawbacks and risks of the synthetic method used by Mr NN. But since no method avoids all risks from the outset and contains only advantages, I believe that, in principle, he cannot be forbidden from using the new method; it is in general terms inevitable today, while in the long run the old method would be far more suspect because it lacks credibility and would simply be rejected by the mind of the more gifted modern students with whom we are concerned.

I assume that Mr NN is sufficiently flexible and self-critical to consider possibly desirable improvements to his teaching method, provided that the essence of that method is accepted. He is right to refuse to teach from a scholastic manual of the old type which has merely been slightly improved and adapted. He is right to believe it is his duty to introduce his pupils to modern problems from the standpoints and principles which are those of modern man and modern science. But I do not believe that Mr NN should conclude from this that his students already have an adequate knowledge of school dogma with all its content (in particular decisions of the teaching authority of the Church) without touching upon the content of scholastic dogma in one way or another. It would perhaps be desirable for him to show greater respect for this content and to make sure that it is assimilated by his audience without replacing this concern by a single declaration that the lecture necessitates advance knowledge of a conventional scholastic manual. I assume that Mr NN would listen to reason on this point.

III. On the Problem of Orthodoxy

1. First a note about the method by which I shall consider the matter of the orthodoxy of this lecture.

(a) On the negative side it must first be stated that it is impossible to give a general analysis of the doctrine contained in these several hundred pages, and to make any theological judgment on the resulting "system" which might perhaps be clearer than in Mr NN's own words. This is simply impossible because the time and space available to me are limited. It is also impossible (and ultimately futile) to extract individual propositions from this work (as though we were concerned with a criticism of Meister Eckhart, Baius or Rosmini), to comment on them and qualify them theologically. Such a procedure would only be justified and possible if a common terminology were available to both parties concerned and the reader as well, together with assumptions and horizons of understanding which would be the same for all concerned, so that critic and reader would immediately understand the sentences they read.

(b) Since these two methods cannot be used here, I can see only one feasible third possibility: an attempt to give the person who will have to reach a practical decision as a higher ecclesiastical authority an initial understanding of Mr NN's objectives, and to urge him to read the work from this standpoint (with the initial understanding gained in this way) before reaching his verdict. I naturally assume—indeed assert—that if this work is read with the necessary initial understanding and from this standpoint, the final judgment will be in Mr NN's favour.

2. Let us assume from the start that this work is inadequate in certain respects which affect its doctrine and are not wholly didactic. What is taken from other disciplines such as exegesis, modern philosophy, contemporary sociology and general science, and then stated, is perhaps, as far as the selection made and the irrefutability of the conclusions drawn are concerned, not so far above all reasonable doubt and possible objections that one might not justifiably wish to have it more appropriately formulated.

The critical reservations apparent in regard to traditional standpoints seem to me no less marked in the work in question than the possibility of offering the same kind of criticism of some trends and standpoints of the disciplines (including modern Protestant exegesis and theology) upon which Mr NN grounds his argument. I entirely grant him the right to choose his authorities according to his own judgment and taste, since that is the only course open to a theologian today. If he invokes a large number of Evangelical exegetes as authorities for his assertions, he is fundamentally entitled to pursue this line, since, after all, the experience of the last fifty years has shown us that Protestant exegetes have very often reached—and very often reach—conclusions which, after more or less fierce opposition, are adopted finally by Catholic exegetes.

However, I would not essentially contest the fact that here and there Mr NN goes too far and offers his audience a somewhat too one-sided kind of critical reservation in respect to the traditional assertions of Catholic scholastic theology. Yet, is there anyone who isn't one-sided? Isn't it true to say that scholastic philosophy to date can be convicted of an extreme ghetto mentality and of indifference even to the point of ignorance in regard to the very sciences which Mr NN so courageously avails himself of? Is this one-sidedness (which, as I have said, affects the doctrine itself to some extent) so considerable that it altogether destroys the

orthodoxy of the material or endangers it to an intolerable degree?
I would think not, if what I say under 3 below is accepted.

3. The starting-point and intention of Mr NN's entire work
must be properly understood if the question of his orthodoxy is to
be answered appropriately.

(a) How has dogmatic theology worked to date? It has simply
taken fundamental theology for granted, and (under the banner
of this merely assumed and never analysed fundamental theology)
has put forward, thought out and systematized the dogmatic propositions derived from the *loci theologici* of the official teaching
of the Church, the Bible and theological tradition, and done so
with the aid of the good or popular philosophy (in the broadest
sense of the word) which was already inherent in these theological
pronouncements of the traditional *loci theologici*, was already
practised in scholastic philosophy, and therefore no longer offered
any particular difficulties. Hence dogmatics was an esoteric discipline to which one gained admission by way of the traditional
kind of fundamental theology: i.e., by way of a fundamental
theology which for its part "proved" the existence of a divine
revelation (above all in Jesus Christ) without itself bothering in
any way about the content of this revelation.

Because this fundamental theology (and of course even more
a largely sociologically conditioned indisputability of faith together with the existing convention of the given formulations of
that faith) led theologians to feel that they were already firmly on
sound dogmatic ground, they were able to practise their theology
in the uncontested and indisputable way familiar to us; that is,
just as a legal expert interprets the legal code whose validity and
meaningfulness he never doubts. This is no longer the case today.
And I am disregarding the fact that fundamental theology (say in
the case of Metz—and quite without regard to the question of his
"political theology") is no longer conceived as that kind of formal
bridge to dogmatic theology, but that its practitioners understand
it as the justification of the content of propositions of belief before
the truth-seeking conscience of contemporary man (and as a
justification which already presupposes dogmatic theology). I also
disregard the fact that such an understanding of fundamental
theology was already established in Thomism proper (say by

Garrigou-Lagrange), even though it could not be directly expressed in exactly this way.

In any case, present-day dogmatics, if it is to be understood and appear credible today, must no longer proceed in this sort of esoteric way. The reason is quite simple: To put it in somewhat summary fashion (and perhaps too roughly): fundamental theology obtains credibility today if the propositions of dogmatic theology obtain credibility, and not the other way round. The difficulty of belief today is to a large extent to be found in the difficulty of assimilating the dogmatic propositions themselves. And it's not—or not *merely*—possible just to assert in reply to that, that in fundamental theology we have already shown that these propositions were revealed and are therefore to be believed even if they seem difficult and obscure, and even if men feel that they really don't know what they have to do with their lives.

In the case of the present philosophical and especially historical difficulties of demonstrating that there was an absolute divine revelation of the word, the difficulty of dogmatic propositions— by way of a kind of feedback effect—implies a difficulty for fundamental theology itself. As a reflex action or instinctively, many people today feel that the assertion that there was a revelation is incredible and extremely doubtful precisely because what is said to have been revealed is extremely incredible and unacceptable, and remains in human consciousness as an incomprehensible relic of earlier stages of human mental development or of a mythology that has now become incomprehensible—a process due to the slowness with which men's consciousness changes in large societies.

In this situation an inner unity of fundamental theology and dogmatics (if these old terms are to be retained at all) is absolutely necessary. Every dogma must, so to speak, be thought out in a "fundamental theological way": that is, it must be demonstrated as meaningful from the basis of its own essential significant content; it must be shown that it has a "place" in men's overall consciousness, and that it can rest on primary human acknowledgment and understanding. Such a possibility exists. It is, so to speak, obstructed in traditional dogmatic school methodology, precisely because this scholasticism sees revelation through peculiarly juridical spectacles as an immense number of individual propositions "positivistically and properly" to be inferred from *the* sources—which themselves exist only in the form of such human (though of course divinely *inspired*) propositions.

But once it is understood that revelation in its original form was something very simple (to be interpreted verbally in a cultural history which is the history of revelation—cf. K. Rahner & J. Ratzinger, *Revelation and Tradition*, London, 1966), it is also understood that in the latter all that is revealed is that the inconceivable mystery of our existence, which rules in and over us and is called God, has promised and devoted itself to an absolutely direct relationship with mankind, and that this covenant is communicated to us with eschatological assurance in Jesus (cf. my remarks on a summary formulation of belief in volumes 8 and 9 of my *Theological Investigations*). Then the legitimacy of the above-mentioned unity of fundamental and dogmatic theology is apparent, together with a dual progression from one to the other of these two: i.e., from dogmatic to fundamental theology and not just the other way round.

(b) From this basis, dogmatics consists essentially on the one hand in an understandable demonstration of the credibility of this quite simple fundamental assertion, and on the other hand in an unfolding of this fundamental assertion in the form of a multitude of traditional dogmatic pronouncements, and in the tracing back of these pronouncements to the fundamental assertion. (For reasons of space, I shall avoid discussion of how ecclesiology and sacramental theology can be essentially included in this conception.) The first task cannot be carried out with the means used by traditional dogmatics, i.e. by the inference of these propositions from the classical *loci theologici*, but occurs in a more original appeal to man's most primal understanding of his existence, to an ultimate will to make sense of things, which is not itself self-enclosed, self-determinate, but experiences itself as sent and endowed, and hence opens itself into the inconceivable mystery of existence, called God, which encounters man in all dimensions of his life ("transcendence", logic and freedom, human relations and future hope). Such an appeal does not transform revelation into natural knowledge, and is not rationalism and mysticism in a bad sense, because on the one hand this derived reference to the directness of absolute mystery is experienced as supported by what theologians call "grace", and hence is itself already "revelation" in a true sense, and because on the other hand this reference realizes itself and communicates itself to itself in what is usually called the history of revelation, and in that (i.e., ultimately in Jesus) finds the ultimate courage to believe (in the form of hope) in its eschatological victory.

(c) If the foregoing is taken into consideration, the absence of any other kind of reference to the "positive sources of revelation" in the case of Mr NN is no longer astonishing. What he wants to achieve is an initial breakthrough to a primary understanding of what is universally and actually said and intended to be said in the texts he discusses, and an initial disclosure of the "location" to which the matter in question is eventually to be assigned; and reciprocally determines his approach by way of both breakthrough and disclosure. He intends no more than this. But what he intends, though modest, is decisive today. If it isn't done, then conventional dogmatics, as practised to date, and supported and determined as self-evident by a socio-traditional Christianity, will in the long run—and precisely by intelligent theologians—be felt to be a mythology which nothing in real life can verify, and which can therefore only at best be tacked on to real life as an incredible and superfluous verbal construct.

(d) On this basis, Mr NN's method also features a certain degree of minimalism. The amount of human data, history and present-day historico-cultural situation needed to discover the "proper location" of a theological assertion in human existence as a given premiss, is perhaps somewhat more narrowly estimated by Mr NN than is strictly necessary, and is perhaps deduced somewhat subjectively from the personal experience and education of Mr NN. But something of the sort is unavoidable, because no one knows everything and has experienced everything, and because exactly the same situation obtains in our traditional scholastic manuals (which no one objects to) to an extent verging on the grotesque and concealed only by the veil of familiarity. In addition, such a limitation of basic assumptions, this kind of methodological minimalism, is particularly justified in *this* very undertaking. The less one has to assume to start with, the better the chance of demonstrating that the theological question and answer are inevitably present in human life. It is justified, too, if this initial methodological minimalism requires a relatively long road (indeed, a longer one compared with earlier premisses) to be taken before the goal aimed at can be reached. Of course it must be presumed in such a case that the teacher really appeals to initial data as presuppositions which are actually taken for granted by his audience in their historico-cultural situation. And I do not think that Mr NN has failed in this respect. In any case, he uses starting-points—even if others might also be invoked—that are absolutely requisite today if a man of our own times is to be clearly shown that there is a relation between his own life and theological propositions such that faith does not appear to be a mere ideological and arbitrary superstructure over and above true reality.

(e) On the basis of these summary indications of the methods used in the work in question and of the foregoing interpretation of revelation, it will be clear that Mr NN avoids taking up an "extrinsic" standpoint not only in his teaching about grace, but in his understanding of revelation, and therefore always tries to derive his starting-point from the "secular nature" of human beings. This has absolutely nothing to do with any kind of modernism (as it existed in the time of Pius X) or with a rationalistic reduction of propositional belief to a purely profane anthropology. To emphasize the secularity of man as a starting-point and as the dimension in which theological propositions have to be justified, is essentially to do no more than to take seriously the fact that grace (as supernatural divinization) and therefore revelation (as the objectification of this very grace) are not *additional* realities to be tacked on to this "secular" man (i.e., man made self-responsible through creation), but are the ultimate radicality and validity of this secularity: i.e., *its* prerequisite.

That this ultimate unity should not cause any denial of a distinction between secular and religious, nature and grace, natural knowledge and revelation, and so on, which is secondary to it though nevertheless legitimate, is precisely a prerequisite of such a method, since secular reality itself is questioned with regard to something that it indicates without itself being that something. Of course one might well ask in regard to Mr NN's work how far in particular instances it succeeds—on the basis of such initial assumptions—in actually attaining to the inherently possible full understanding of propositional belief. This problem could be dealt with by examining each individual assertion critically. Yet care must be taken not to reject too speedily as false or inadequate unconventional "translations" and interpretations of traditional theological pronouncements which Mr NN arrives at on the basis of his premiss and by his method, i.e., to reject them because they are unconventional and therefore are disadvantaged in comparison with traditional propositions—which to a large extent we think are so clear, definite and illuminating merely because we are used to them.

In conclusion, I must say that I have learned a lot from these lectures. I have learned a lot precisely because on first reading them I was very often shocked. Should one "pan" their author?

First of all, we have to remember that the situation in which— and therefore the criteria by which—we judge a theologian today have to be quite different to those usual in our circles twenty years ago. Earlier on, when a particular theologian's approach engendered suspicion of his heterodoxy or evoked a judgment of insecure theology, he could be rejected without any consequent damage to the teaching of the Church itself. For this teaching existed in an environment in which our theology was universally prevalent, and in the consciousness of those to whom it tried to speak, as a certainty that was not open to refutation.

Today this teaching of the Church is very largely disputed as a fact in the very environment in which theology lives and speaks, even though a good number of the older theologians in our ranks have not yet adverted to or do not wish to advert to this actuality. In this situation, the existence of a theologian who ultimately wishes to serve the Church's teaching, is already a significant positive factor, even if such a theologian does not, in respect to this or that particular point, fully succeed in satisfactorily answering his intention of producing an acceptable expression of the Church's teaching. He bears witness to the teaching of the Church even though the clear intention to do so is not successful in every individual instance. A professor of this kind, who in the eyes of his students emphatically addresses himself to the contemporary spiritual situation and its problems, ultimately contributes more to the strengthening of his audience's faith than does a professor who exhibits a ghettolike and sterile orthodoxy.

Of course, it might be said that a professor should display both modernity and an appropriate orthodoxy. But such lucky cases in which *both* requirements are wholly satisfied occur very seldom. If we want professors who seriously raise new questions, we just have to reckon with a calculated risk. This does not mean that Mr NN, despite all good intentions, has actually gone beyond the bounds of orthodoxy at one or the other point. But what I have just remarked on must also be taken into consideration if a proficient decision is to be reached in regard to the whole question. Any attempt to resolve the question by appointing another professor to satisfy the needs of the bulk of his existing audience, and merely using Mr NN for graduates writing doctoral theses and theologians of similar scholastic attainment is out. Among all theologians, whatever the level of their intelligence or the stage of their education, the problems are essentially the same.

If the present-day situation means that the "shrewder" students need a professor like Mr NN, then the others need a teacher of the same mould. For the "others" suffer the same difficulties, even though they are able to articulate them less precisely and therefore give the impression that they can be fobbed off with a less proficient mentor.

I seem to have written something approaching a treatise. I realize that I've stayed on a very general level—as I said I would at the beginning. But a discussion of the points of detail at issue would have needed something like half the length of a normal book on the subject, which I'm not in a position to offer you. Anyway, all detailed exposition on behalf of Mr NN would be significant and have any chance of success only if the general considerations which I've put forward already were all accepted. But in that case, I think, a positive solution to the NN case would be arrived at without any detailed treatise of individual propositions. And a positive judgment is what I sincerely hope will be the outcome.

With best wishes,
Yours . . . .

Translated by John Griffiths

PART II
BULLETIN

Michael Raske / Ludwig Rütti / Klaus Schäfer

Attempts to Realize
Human Rights within the Church

Aims of the Solidarity Action Groups in German-speaking Countries

GROUPS of Catholic priests have established themselves in practically every diocese of Federal Germany as well as in Austria and Switzerland.[1] Initially these groups, formed for various reasons

[1] General bibliography: *Eine freie Kirche für eine freie Welt*. Documentation commissioned by the study group of priest groups (AGP) in the Federal Republic and edited by M. Raske, K. Schäfer, N. Wetzel (Düsseldorf, 1969) (whence further literature); *Impulse zur Freiheit. Initiativen der Solidaritätsgruppen zur Kirchenreform*. Documentation commissioned by AGP and edited by G. Saltin (Düsseldorf; to appear in 1971); programme of a spontaneous group critical of the Church, *Orientierung* 33 (1969), pp. 113–15; M. Raske, "Rebellen oder Hirten? Struktur, Motive und Ziele katholischer Priestergruppen in der Bundesrepublik", in *Publik* (30.1.1970), p. 24; by the same: "Reform und Solidarität. Zur Situation katholischer Priestergruppen", in *Wissenschaft und Praxis in Kirche und Gesellschaft* 59 (1970), pp. 237–45; K. Schäfer, "Zum Thema Priestergruppen", in *Stimmen der Zeit* 95 (1970), pp. 43–6; reply to this article by K. Rahner, "Chancen der Priestergruppen", *loc. cit.*, pp. 172–80; in answer to this again K. Schäfer, "Nochmals: Zum Thema Priestergruppen", *loc. cit.*, pp. 361–78 (the three contributions were reprinted in a special issue of *SOG-Papiere* 3 [1970], pp. 242–80); the same, "Zur Situation der Priestergruppen in der BRD", in *SOG-Papiere* 3 (1970), pp. 181–5; information concerning the work of Protestant reform groups in *ad hoc: Kritische Kirche*, documentation, edited by D. Lange, R. Leudesdorff a.o. (Gelnhausen, 1969); regular publications worth mentioning: *Für eine offene Kirche*, Informationsdienst kritischer Gruppen (Zürich, Steinwiesstr. 6); *Imprimatur*, Meinungen Nachrichten, Kritik aus der Trierer Kirche, edited by the study circle imprimatur (Trier, Blankensteinstr. 11); in particular *SOG-Papiere*, Mitteilungsblatt der Arbeitsgemeinschaft von Priestergruppen in der BRD und der SOG Oesterreich (Bochum, Postfach 926).

and in varying conditions, had more or less limited ideas, aims and activities. However, in a short time intensive national and international collaboration led to the realization that these activities must be carried on in a more comprehensive historical, ecclesiological and theological framework. This development is continuing; in German-speaking countries it is largely characterized by the slogan: "Human rights within the Church". This suggests a sociological and ecclesiological outlook which determines all activities and involves a new ecclesiological position.

I

The majority of these priest groups in German-speaking countries were set up in 1968/9. Four years after the end of Vatican II it is becoming increasingly evident that both spirit and impetus of the Council are being suppressed by a new "Counter-reformation" (J. B. Metz). Parish priests and curates are finding the discrepancy they experience every day between modern demands for Christian responsibility and the reactionary mentality of churchmen and Church institutions intolerable. Hence these solidarity groups quickly transcended the specifically professional problems of the priesthood.

It was already stated in the "manifesto" of the "Study Group of Priest Groups in Federal Germany" (AGP) that it is a question of a radical change in outlook, by which the Church must catch up on the historical development of modern society. "In order to bridge the gap the Church must at least incorporate in its institutions those safeguards of human liberty which, during the last two centuries, were won in the political field in the struggle against an open or veiled abuse of power (fundamental rights, distribution of power, and control of policy-making)."[2] That the Church lags behind with regard to human rights is evident. It does not see "human rights" as grounded in "natural law" and hence deducible from abstract principles, but as historical trophies wrested during the course of enlightenment and emancipation from the feudal and hierarchical powers of State and Church.

In Federal Germany—where the situation differs from that in

[2] *Eine freie Kirche*, pp. 42 ff.

Romance countries and Latin America—there is no widespread revolutionary consciousness either in society or in the Church. Hence the solidarity groups' advocacy of human rights within the Church will appear at first hand as a demand for "liberalization". This can be explained by the situation of the Church in Federal Germany. Generally speaking, there is no conflict between it and the State or society as a whole. Its network of parishes is functioning. Thanks to the Church tax its bureaucracy is increasingly independent of parish grass roots. Through religious education in schools being guaranteed by the State and the existence of State theological faculties it possesses a huge apparatus of religious instruction; furthermore, numerous institutions for the theological training of adults, an elaborate Church press and a great number of charitable organizations. Within certain limits discussions are possible.

Some reforms, e.g., the renewal of the liturgy and the establishment of councils, are carried out on a comparatively broad basis. Here the clergy have chiefly been trained at theological faculties; their education has been fairly liberal. Only rarely have they a personal knowledge of financial hardship. Normally any attempt to break out of this practically comprehensive system will involve the loss of all influence since the individual would find himself in a social no-man's-land.

On the other hand, this system still seems to offer a possible basis for reform. However, in such a situation the sensitiveness to hidden, yet effective and far-reaching forms of prejudice and oppression in society as well as in the Church could easily be blunted; e.g., in some places access to information and public discussions concerning significant problems and events (the Pastoral Council in the Netherlands, Church tax, the law of celibacy, the indissolubility of marriage, birth control, the so-called Dutch catechism for adults) were almost completely blocked.[3] Spontaneous demands for general questionnaires met with opposition;[4] after prolonged delaying tactics the effect of such questionnaires was finally impaired by the vagueness of the questions set; initially any formation of critical groups and units was

[3] A documented example in *Imprimatur* 3 (1970/4), pp. 18 ff.
[4] For example, the questionnaire of AGP concerning discussions about celibacy in December 1968, *SOG-Papiere* 2 (1969/1), pp. 17 ff.

on principle suspected as constituting a danger to the Church; the simple rights of participation in policy-making are still withheld; the question of the election of bishops and the statute for the General Synod of the German dioceses, which the German Episcopal Conference decided upon in the face of strong protests, are clear cases in point.[5] There is moral and legal discrimination against mixed marriages, divorced and re-married Christians, and married priests.[6] Catholics who reject the present system of Church taxation and withdraw from it are threatened with excommunication.[7]

In the eyes of critical groups this situation is ambivalent. They can work within the framework of official organizations where they have a relatively wider scope than similar groups in Southern Europe or Latin America. However, in this way their work will have no short-term effects and direct action be handicapped. Above all, such groups always run the danger of becoming victims of their own surroundings. Consequently they may not only base their choice of methods on their own special situation but also lower their aims, losing sight of the historical nexus and the demands of the historical situation.

For this reason it has become increasingly evident that the significance and urgency of a programme envisaging the realization of human rights within the Church cannot be understood nor, in the last resort, upheld unless it is connected with the

[5] Cf. corresponding analyses in *Demokratisierung der Kirche in der Bundesrepublik Deutschland*. Memorandum of German Catholics, edited by the Bamberger Kreis (Mainz, 1970), and *In Sachen Synode. Vorschläge und Argumente des Vorbereitungskongresses*, edited by N. Greinacher, K. Lang, P. Scheuermann (Düsseldorf, 1970).

[6] A series of discriminations concerning mixed marriages documented in *Mischehe. Materialdienst des Arbeitskreises Mischehe Würzburg* (Reichenberg), and W. and M. R. Will (editors), *Wir leben in Mischehe*. Protestant and Catholic partners speaking in order to help (Munich, 1969). Concerning the position of the divorced, cf. N. Wetzel (editor), *Die öffentlichen Sünder oder Soll die Kirche Ehen scheiden* (Mainz, 1970). Results of research into the situation of priests who change their profession or marry are about to be published; cf. *SOG-Papiere* 2 (1969/1), pp. 40 ff. (Publication of secret instructions by the former Holy Office), cf. *ibid.*, pp. 14 ff., 56, 60 ff.; *loc. cit.* 2 (1969/4), pp. 49 ff., 75 ff.; *loc. cit.* 3 (1970), pp. 2 ff. (concerning the exceptionally difficult situation in East Germany), pp. 136 ff.

[7] Cf. Position of AGP regarding the declaration of Catholic bishops on questions of Church finance, *SOG-Papiere* 3 (1970), p. 318.

problem of Church and society. The fact that men are kept in tutelage and are denied elementary rights and liberties in the Church, and the attitude ·of the hierarchy in ecclesio-political questions have a social significance at home and abroad.

Since the international conference in Amsterdam (28 Sept.– 4 Oct. 1970)[8] it has been realized that the difference between the groups from various countries can no longer simply be accounted for by any differences in their situations. In fact, there are manifold and effective connections between Church and society in the Federal Republic and its counterparts in countries like Spain, Portugal[9] and the Latin-American States. "Guest" workers and the "third world" make us see that Church and society in the Federal Republic are involved in the world-wide system of oppression and exploitation.

II

The fact that there is a growing solidarity in the historical process of enlightenment and emancipation to which these action groups feel responsible and within which they are fighting for the realization of human rights within the Church, also has an ecclesiological significance.[10] The suppression of changes which were long overdue and adumbrated by Vatican II has led to spontaneous action for collective self-help. This challenges an institutional Church, whose hierarchical organization isolates the individual—especially the cleric—and surrenders him, thus isolated, to a higher authority in order to manifest the unity of the clergy or at least to sustain this fiction in public.

It is the very existence and activity of the basic groups of priests and lay people which revealed that even new words like "collegiality", "co-responsibility" and "dialogue" can be used

[8] Cf. U. Schwarz, "Erwachen in Amsterdam", in *Publik* (16 Oct. 1970), p. 24.
[9] Cf. *Der totalitäre Gottesstaat. Die Lage der Christen in Portugal, Spanien und im Baskenland*. Documentation, commissioned by AGP and edited by M. Raske, K. Schäfer, N. Wetzel (Düsseldorf, 1970).
[10] Cf. K. Derksen, "Solidarisierung innerhalb der Kirche", in *Orientierung* 33 (1969), pp. 132–5; M. Raske, K. Schäefer, N. Wetzel, "Gruppenbildungen in der Kirche—warum und wozu?", in *SOG-Papiere* 3 (1970), pp. 188–90; O. Schreuder, *Revolution in der Kirche? Kritik der kirchlichen Amtsstruktur* (Das theologische Interview 3) (Düsseldorf, 1969).

as means and simultaneously ideological camouflage for continuing repression. The objection to "dialogue" made by Church officials and conservatives that these spontaneous groups are not representative of the clergy, because they can neither claim a status sanctioned by canon law nor a numerical majority, is typical.[11]

However, in the present situation the criterion of being representative—at least when taken as the sole one—is questionable. "Is it not possible that, while only answering for their few members, these groups are actually speaking for great numbers, for entire strata which are inarticulate in the life of the Church? Who represents the excommunicated, the disappointed, those who have outgrown their 'milieu', those numerous Christians who do not identify themselves with the norms, values, doctrines and rites of the Church? Who speaks vicariously for Christians who expose themselves to changes in the apprehension of the Faith and are thus forced to ask and experience what words like 'God' might mean? Which group among 'committed' Christians are consciously trying not only to think about the 'anonymous Christians' and those who are being prevented from becoming Christians, but to stand in for these people within the Church?"[12]

By forming groups and collaborating internationally the growing solidarity movement does not only aim at ensuring a stronger position against the hierarchy and administration and so to promote the emancipation of those directly involved. It is mainly concerned with those people whose problems and experiences are outside the scope of or contradict the mentality, institutions and ideologies of the Church. Hence the attempt to transcend the limits of the official Church. The needs and challenges of today are forcing us to go beyond our set nationalized and institutionalized Christianity and to include not only the more comprehensive Christian tradition, but also the fundamental human experiences of the present day in our religious responsibilities.

In this way the groups seek to foster the awareness of the actual difference between being a Christian and being member of the

---

[11] Reply of K. Rahner, "Droht ein Schisma in der katholischen Kirche?", in *Stimmen der Zeit* 94 (1969), pp. 20–33, esp. pp. 29 ff.

[12] K. Schäfer, "Zum Thema Priestergruppen", in *Stimmen der Zeit*, *loc. cit.*, p. 38.

Church, and to make this critical awareness effective in changing the Church. That is why for the groups there is no fundamental dilemma between a critical involvement "inside" or "outside" the Church. "Is it not possible that in the future for many Catholics the attempt to identify themselves with the cause of Christ, i.e., to become Christians, can only be realized as a process of emancipation and that for many this emancipation will be the only alternative to resignation, visible break with the Church or inner emigration, in fact the way to Christian liberty?"[13] For the priest groups in German-speaking countries this emancipation is at present mainly embodied in their attempts to realize human rights within the Church.

III

The concrete aims, declarations and actions of these priest groups are directed towards the realization of human rights primarily as they promote the personal integrity and liberty of the individual and endeavour to change institutions and their attitudes for this purpose. Using the slogan "democratization" and "humanization" in the settlement of actual problems and controversies, they aim at curtailing the power of arbitrary and disfunctional authority and consequently liberating men from their tutelage and reliance on authority, from fear and guilt complexes caused by unjust laws and authoritarian attitudes.[14]

The Church must be given a constitution in which elementary human rights are grounded.[15] By distribution of power and the setting up of independent courts all insecurity before the law must be eliminated.[16] Legal proceedings must be standardized so that the individual is protected from arbitrariness, discrimination and inhuman harshness: especially in the case of matrimonial

[13] *Ibid.*, p. 40.
[14] Cf. "Gegenwärtige Probleme und soziale Position des Weltgeistlichen", Socio-psychological study commissioned by North German Ordinaries, but not published; published in extracts in *SOG-Papiere* 1 (1968/1), pp. 35–42; *loc. cit.* 2 (1969/1), pp. 30–9; cf. L. Hoffmann, "Der frustrierte Klerus. Ueber einige Erfahrungen junger Priester", in *Katechetische Blätter* 93 (1968), pp. 597–610.
[15] Cf. "Römische Breschnew-Doktrin", in *Imprimatur* 3 (1970/6), pp. 8–11, *id.*, *SOG-Papiere* 3 (1970), pp. 281–4.
[16] Cf. *SOG-Papiere* 2 (1969/5), pp. 65 ff.; *loc. cit.* 3 (1970), pp. 315 ff.

courts, trials concerning orthodoxy and the procedures for laicization.[17]

The struggle of priest groups in Federal Germany against unjust and inhuman laws was exemplified in their attack on the laws, regulations and procedures connected with "mixed marriages". Even after revision these remain in some respects unjustifiable both theologically and by the situation of the Christians they affect. They transgress against freedom of conscience and the personal responsibility of the marriage partners. They still discriminate against non-Catholic Churches and Christians, subjecting them to unnecessary and degrading measures (dispensations, *sanatio in radice*).[18]

Nor can the question of those "re-married in the Christian parish community" be delayed any longer. "From the pastoral point of view the practical exclusion of so many married couples from the Church is an irresponsible scandal. It prevents these couples from coming to terms with a sad fate in a humane and Christian fashion, and imposes an intolerable burden on them. Not infrequently is the priest forced to advocate the position of traditional canon law against his own theological and pastoral conscience."[19]

The question of the indissolubility of marriage must be subject to theological re-thinking (why does canon law only acknowledge the divorce of valid marriages in consideration of *bonum fidei*, i.e., in the interests of the Church, and not in consideration of *bonum hominis?*) and allowances made for changes in society.

[17] Cf. note 6, *supra*.

[18] Resolution of AGP concerning mixed marriages, *Eine freie Kirche*, pp. 48–52; *SOG-Papiere* 2 (1969/4), pp. 61 ff., reprinted in P. Lengsfeld, *Das Problem Mischehe. Einer Lösung entgegen* (Freiburg, 1970), pp. 195–204. Commentaries: Gesslerhut, *Imprimatur* 3 (1970/6), pp. 1 ff., "Oekumenischer Fortschritt oder Vereinfachung der Verwaltung", *loc. cit.* 3 (1970/8), pp. 1 ff., and "Aktionsvorschläge", in *SOG-Papiere* 3 (1970), pp. 196 ff., 280, in which the refusal to continue applying for dispensations in cases of different denominations was announced, met with criticism from the bishops, *loc. cit.*, p. 199, *Imprimatur* 3 (1970/8), pp. 19 ff. However, they led to a general easing up of implementary regulations for dispensations by German bishops.

[19] *Eine freie Kirche*, p. 53; cf. *SOG-Papiere* 2 (1969/4), pp. 68 ff., reprinted in N. Wetzel, *Die öffentlichen Sünder, op. cit.*, pp. 271 ff. *Ibid.*, pp. 164 ff. for further reflections and reports on the novel practice.

The "democratization" of information, the search for truth and of decision-making is meant to guarantee the fundamental rights to free opinion and co-responsibility. "In order to be able to protest against the degradation of men in totalitarian systems and in an overplanned world and to advocate liberty as a condition of peace, it (the Church) must itself fundamentally democratize its institutions in a theologically legitimate sense, i.e., in the search for truth and in all decision-making expertise, publicity and co-responsibility of all concerned must be realized as principles of Christian action."[20]

This democratization is not a matter of fashionable adaptation to existing sociological patterns, but of the credibility and efficacy of Christian witness in present world conditions. It is equally demanded with regard to the choice of officials, the effective control of their administration and the genuine competence of elected bodies (Councils, Synods).[21] Finally, it is necessary for a community, in which individuals are respected as mature and responsible people, to be allowed the formation of groups and societies, the fostering of critical public opinion, and the open and reasonable settlement of conflicts.

Although the priest groups are not primarily concerned with pressing demands for themselves, they must also advocate a free choice of profession and of living standards.[22] For this demand implies a change in that fundamental outlook and mentality the disastrous effects of which reach far beyond the personal problems of priests.

The examples quoted should elucidate how the solidarity groups in German-speaking countries are working for the

[20] Manifesto "Basiserklärung" of AGP, *Eine freie Kirche*, p. 43.

[21] Cf. "Neustrukturierung der Kirche. Drei Voten aus dem jungen deutschen Diözesanklerus", in *Diakonia* 3 (1968), pp. 284–99; G. Biemer, "Die Bischofswahl als neues Desiderat kirchlicher Praxis", in *Tübinger Theol. Quartalschrift* 149 (1969), pp. 171–84; cf. *SOG-Papiere* 2 (1969/4), pp. 71, 75 ff.; e.g., trial elections caused violent opposition in Paderborn, cf. *loc. cit.* 3 (1970), pp. 114 ff.; cf. *Demokratisierung der Kirche. op. cit.*

[22] Cf. concerning the question of further professional education *SOG-Papiere* 2 (1969/4), p. 50; free choice of profession, *Eine freie Kirche*, pp. 59 ff.; free choice of celibacy or marriage, *loc. cit.*, pp. 58 ff., *SOG-Papiere* 3 (1970), pp. 30 ff.; concerning further employment of married priests in the service of the Church, *SOG-Papiere* 2 (1969/4), pp. 50 ff., *loc. cit.* 3 (1970), pp. 194 ff. (Aktionsvorschläge).

realization of human rights within the Church. It may be too soon to decide whether this method will be successful. Hitherto, combined with the co-operation of groups from other European countries and the "third world", it has led men to recognize the interaction of Church and social activities. In future this may bring about a change to more detailed analyses of sociological patterns, not in order to escape ecclesiological problems, but to find a *pou sto* for Christian responsibility and thereby gain a valid perspective for inner-Church problems.

Translated by Irene Marinoff

Walter Hollenweger

Criteria for Reforming the Church

Based on Material presented by the so-called
Action-Research Groups

"In the course of her history the Church has at least twice
experienced the shattering of her traditional ecclesiological
concepts—during the Apostolic Age, when pagans were
converted to Christianity without having become members
of the Jewish People first, and in the fourth century, when
the emperor, the head and representative of the unbeliev-
ing world power, became a Christian while remaining
emperor. In both cases the reason for this was that the
missionary preaching of the Church had found an echo in
unexpected quarters. Both times theology was challenged:
during the Apostolic Age St Paul and the Early Christians
found a solution which was, at least in its main points,
common. Today we are still confronted with the task of
explaining the situation of the Church in the world,
heralded in the fourth century, in theological terms; for in
the present ecumenical dialogue and faced with the situation of Christians throughout the world, the position of the
Reformation must be stated afresh."[1]

THIS is G. Kretschmar's diagnosis of the ecclesiological situation
today. We may agree with his conclusion—that the position of the
Reformation must be stated afresh—or not. He certainly makes
one point clear: that ecclesia precedes ecclesiology and not vice
versa. This is really a truism, but over and over again forgotten.

[1] G. Kretschmar, "Der Weg zur Reichskirche", in *Verkündigung und
Forschung* (*Beih. Ev. Theol.* 13, 1968), pp. 43 ff.

Actual History precedes the History of Ideas

Today the discrepancy between the teaching about the Church and the reality of the Church has increased to such an extent that e.g. in his superb analysis of the "significance of the Pentecostal Movement for the Catholic Church"[2] the *regional* of the Brazilian Episcopal Conference and collaborator of Helder Cämara, Abdalazis de Moura, could put the question: How is it possible that, without a corresponding ecclesiology, these Pentecostal Christians could develop an ecclesiastical *practice* which is analogous to what our best contemporary theologians are still only *thinking*, but cannot yet put into practice?

The same phenomenon also occurs in other fields. While the influence of the Church is on the wane, there is an increasing interest in theological problems, theological books, films and radio programmes not only in Europe but also in socialist countries and in the third world. This is at the same time disturbing and gratifying. Furthermore, theological problems are arising in non-Christian cultures, and new Christian Churches are being founded that call themselves Christian without accepting any of our ecclesiologies or, in some cases, any form of baptism.

This problem was tackled from various angles in research projects carried out by the Ecumenical Council, e.g., there was a comprehensive survey of fifteen Churches in as differing situations as Hamburg and Chile, or India and Great Britain. When comparing these different Churches hitherto no systematically satisfying categories could be found.[3] Beyond that, phenomena were even discovered which, in our present habitual categories, could only be described in mutually exclusive terms. (This may be a hint that the law of opposites does not possess the general validity hitherto ascribed to it.) The study ended with the unsatisfactory reference to "a very humble agnosticism" with regard to ecclesiological statements, which may be "humble", but can by no means be called sufficient.

[2] A. de Moura, "Importância das Igrejas Pentecostais para a Igreja Católica" (duplicated, Rua Jiriquiti 48, Boa Vista, Recife).

[3] All English copies obtainable from the World Council of Churches, Geneva (1958–1970). *The Growth of the Church in Buganda. An Attempt at Understanding*, by John V. Taylor (London, 1958); "Can Churches be Compared? Reflections on fifteen study projects" by St Mackie, *Research Pamphlet* 17 (Geneva and New York, 1970).

Pluriformity in the Church

Hoekendijk approaches the problem in a different way. His solution is pluriformity of the Church. "Ecclesiastical pluralism implies (if necessary) the continued existence of contradictory forms of congregational life with completely differing social comprehensiveness and morphology. Instances of such co-existing types are: 'Institutions of permanent supply' (Kortzfleisch), exclusively occupied with providing 'services' without envisaging the formation of parishes; traditional parishes, which will probably only find a clear-cut profile once they are freed from their illusions of monopoly and have delegated an essential part of their present functions to other bodies; institutions of permanent communities with strictly disciplined congregational life, as e.g., the numerous 'ordoid' communities (Taizé a.o.), among these small domestic groups, and of late many 'team' or 'group-ministries'; study groups entrusted with a strictly limited mandate and then dissolving, etc. In advance none of these structures is excluded or disqualified as incomplete. Only practice will show what can be utilized."[4] It cannot be denied that a number of such Church types exist today.

In this connection Hoekendijk refers to the report of the North American working group of the Department on Studies in Evangelism. "Here, especially in North America, this idea of a missionary Church in a pluralistic society has been firmly outlined against the background of an efficient action-research."[5]

This may be a helpful description of the Church in "action", however "research" has not yet been sufficiently envisaged. We are only at the beginning of our thinking, reflection and intellectual reassembling of facts; for the question how they are all related is ineluctable.

Chances and Dangers of Nomenclature

Although, in my opinion, it is too soon to consider the attempts to subsume the above-mentioned data under an ecclesiological system, as a failure, the simple fact remains that this ecclesiology

[4] J. Chr. Hoekendijk, *Kirche und Volk in der deutschen Missionswissenschaft* (Munich, 1967), pp. 352–3; abbreviated German translation of *Kerk en Volk in de Duitse Zendingswetenschap* (Amsterdam, 1948).

[5] Hoekendijk, *op. cit.*, p. 353.

has been unsuccessful both in the ecumenical and the denominational dialogue. Of course, one can take one's stand on a denominational point of view, judging the above-mentioned Church types by the Lutheran, Reformed or Catholic doctrinal positions considered as valid interpretations of the Bible. However, this valuation overlooks the fact that the pluralism of New Testament ecclesiologies (E. Schweizer and E. Käsemann) precludes such a judgment. Besides, Church life in one's own denomination very often no longer corresponds to the ecclesiologies accepted there.

Finally, at least till the formulation of the so-called Apostles' Creed, the unity of the Early Church did not consist in a creed, and certainly not in an ecclesiology, but in common hymns, common stories (later called tradition) and the almost "sacramental" journeys of St Paul to collect money. Today, too, Christians are not united by creeds or ecclesiologies, but e.g. by the Lord's Prayer, certain songs, at times certain actions and possibly also collections.

Maybe—though I only dare to voice the thought in the shape of a question—there are things that should not be given a name. "To quote criteria" and to "label" has indeed become a necessity in our civilization. At the same time this has strangled the immediacy of experience. It is no coincidence that in many ancient fairy tales pronouncing a name means death (Rumpelstiltskin).

Today our situation is similar to the one described by Kretschmar. I am unable to judge whether this is due to the success of Christian missionary activities or whether these Churches originated in spite of our missions, or to both. The fact remains that in the so-called independent Churches in Africa and Latin America as well as among the "latent Christians", the free functional groups in Europe and America "another Church" is coming into being which can only with difficulty be included in our ecclesiological categories.

[6] Th. Wieser (ed.), *Planning For Mission. Working Papers on the New Quest for Missionary Communities* (Geneva and New York, 1966)—*The Church for Others and the Church for the World. A Quest for Structures for Missionary Congregations.* Final Report of the Western European Working Group and North American Working Group of the Department on Studies in Evangelism (Geneva, 1969[4])—W. J. Hollenweger, "The

Alternatives to Conceptual Systematization

This situation is the starting-point for the ecumenical thought-and-action study programme: "The Structure of the Missionary Congregation". One might ask: "What continuing elements unite the traditional Churches with this other Church? What systematical categories can include phenomena as diverse as the Eglise de Jésus Christ sur la terre par le prophète Simon Kibangu in the Congo,[7] the Igreja Evangélica Pentecostal in Brazil,[8] the independent Churches in Africa,[9] the political nocturnal prayer in Cologne,[10] the Sjaloom-groups in Holland,[11] the Mississippi-Delta Service in the Southern States of the United States of America,[12] the Metropolitan Association in Philadelphia,[13] a Lenten service during Passiontide in Puerto Rico?[14] Where are the categories simultaneously to embrace these and the traditional Churches? Can both types be termed Churches in the same sense, and why? Does a border-line between orthodoxy and heresy still exist, and if so, by which categories can it be determined? Doctrinal ones? —but if many of these Churches refrain from presenting their teaching in systematic form?; liturgical ones?—but if all liturgies, even the traditional ones, are in flux?; attachment to the Bible?— that might be a useful criterion, provided it could be explained

---

Church for Others, Discussion in the DDR", in *Study Encounter* 5/1 (1969), pp. 26–36; currently: *Monthly Letter on Evangelism* (Geneva) and *Concept*.

[7] Cf. a book about to be published by Marie-Louise Martin (Basle, Reinhardt).

[8] M. de Melo, "The Church that has Nothing More to Give. Evangelism from the point of view of a Brazilian Pentecostalist", *Monthly Letter on Evangelism* (Geneva, 1969); W. J. Hollenweger, *Enthusiastisches Christentum. Die Pfingstbewegung in Geschichte und Gegenwart* (Zürich and Wuppertal, 1969).

[9] V. E. W. Hayward (ed.) "African Independent Church Movements", *Research Pamphlets* 11 (Geneva, 1963).

[10] D. Sölle and F. Steffensky, *Politisches Nachtgebet in Köln* (Stuttgart, 1969²).

[11] H. J. Herbort, "Catholics in Holland Introduce Bold Changes. Liturgical reform in full swing", *Monthly Letter on Evangelism*, May/June 1967.

[12] H. Hellstern, *Mississippi* (Basle, 1969); B. Hilton, *The Delta Ministry* (New York and London, 1969).

[13] "The Church for Others", *loc. cit.*, pp. 108–16.

[14] E. H. Osorio, "Is Fasting a Form of Evangelism? A symbolic action and its interpretation in Puerto Rico", *Monthly Letter on Evangelism*, June/Sept. 1969.

equally well to the illiterate as to the literate what attachment to the Bible means; confession of "the Lord Jesus Christ as God and Saviour in accordance with Holy Scripture" as the basic formula of the Ecumenical Council expresses it—but is this formula sufficient, when it is left unsaid what loyalties to other "gods and saviours" (political, ideological, racist, cultural, economic) are excluded by this confession?

Is this argument a defence of muddled thinking in favour of an ecclesiology which is vaguely felt, but cannot be cast in systematic form? That would not be enough. However, I am attempting something which may be termed unscientific in our latitudes, but which I nevertheless call a scientific approach because it is appropriate. Instead of mentioning *abstract criteria* I am going to describe *how criteria originate*, by taking the Eucharistic banquet as an example.

The Eucharistic Banquet as "communio oppositorum"

In the Eucharistic banquet the *communio oppositorum*, postulated theoretically by Hoekendijk, is celebrated. It is forward-looking, outward-going and open towards others. It is evident that a Eucharist, which is conceived in this way, can no longer be bound by confessional limitations. Yet this is no plea for inter-communion (the word itself is a contradiction in terms). It demands new eucharistic rites, in which the divisory forces such as rich and poor, coloured and white, men and women, children and adults, intellectuals and illiterate, socialists and capitalists, which are *effective in our midst*, are transcended by the celebration. Already in the Early Church a community (e.g. between slaves and free men), which was only just beginning to emerge, was anticipated eschatologically. This does not mean that opposites should be blunted or harmonized, but the search for hitherto unknown alternatives. Particularly in the eucharistic feast *"sola gratia"* is applied to thought processes.[15] Whenever the struggle for truth is carried on within the horizons of hope—not of resignation and obstinate sticking to one's point, i.e., at the table of the Lord, new alternatives can emerge. These are not blockaded by our need "to be right". There is no longer any need to justify

[15] W. J. Hollenweger, "Spiel als eine Form von Theologie. Zum geplanten Dialog mit der Pfingstbewegung", *Luth. Monatshefte* (Oct. 1970), pp. 532–4.

ourselves, as we are already justified. So it is not necessary to defend antiquated positions for the sake of being right. Discussions around the table of the Lord are not about truth, but directed towards the truth. Communion understood as a process of searching for knowledge is of supreme significance, because truth is definitely not a matter of democracy, but fundamentally the gift of him who is present in the midst of the *communio oppositorum* and makes this *communio* possible. To be sure there is only one truth. But as soon as I define truth, it becomes particular, for by definition any definition divides, while by definition the *communio oppositorum* unites.... In this forward-looking community *agalliasis*, the joy of the Early Christians, has its place as well as a sense of humour, which relativizes one's own particular truth."[16] As Bonhoeffer wrote from prison, "Final seriousness is never without a pinch of humour."[17]

Forward-looking involves outward-going. It was a revolutionary action of the first Christians to carry, as they did, the bread, the "Body of Christ", out into the world, when the hungry Corinthians were fed with the "Body broken for many".[18] Here no separation was made between the hunger of the stomach and the hunger of the heart. "Which other religious group would have, at that time, used their Holy of Holies to satisfy the ordinary hunger of the body? Which religious community today is prepared to surrender their Holy of Holies to this world?"[19]

Being open towards others is not only shown in sustaining differences of opinion. "Here it is a question of 'resisting' each other 'to the face' (Gal. 2. 11) in the name of brotherliness, but face to face, not behind the back! The style of dialogue which the Lord enables us to carry on at his Table, and which, at the same time, he requires from us, does not mean a compromise, but the search for what transcends the opposites. This apparent impossibility can be expressed, because the Lord himself sits at the table with us, because we are not only among brothers, because

[16] W. Simpfendörfer, *Offene Kirche, kritische Kirche. Kirchenreform am Scheideweg* (Stuttgart, 1969), pp. 163-4.

[17] D. Bonhoeffer, *Widerstand und Ergebung* (Munich, 1966[13]), p. 256.

[18] Cf. Th. Klauser, *Kleine abendländische Liturgiegeschichte. Bericht und Besinnung* (Bonn, 1965). W. J. Hollenweger, "Liturgiereform als Sozialreform", *Neues Forum* (Vienna, 1969), pp. 711-13.

[19] W. Simpfendörfer, *op. cit.*, p. 163.

we are not 'brothers in spite of everything', but because we are called brothers by him."[20]

Being open towards others largely depends on the style of leadership in the Church, on the office of bishop, whether he be called president, moderator, bishop, vicar or priest. "His office is not primarily one of government, but mobilization of hope. As a bishop of the open Church he is 'not Lord of the Faith, but promoter of joy' (Phil. 4). Thus he does not stand 'above the parties', does not move 'beyond good and evil' nor is he simply 'the man of compromise'. By advocating a fearless realism and promoting an appealing concretization of the Gospel, he creates and defends the climate of joy and the atmosphere of openness.

"But what does the bishop do when the partakers of the banquet begin to quarrel? Does he settle the dispute? Does he seek a compromise? Does he dismiss the indecent and wayward from the table (Church discipline)? What means does he employ to perform his function? If the attitude of Jesus were the pattern for bishops, we certainly do not find him dismissing those who do not conform, 'the publicans and sinners' from his table. When he had been kissed and anointed in an unusual fashion by a sinner in the house of Simon the Pharisee and was challenged to pass judgment, he told the parable of the two debtors which ends with a question. That is to say he placed the conflict in a wider—today we would say 'theological'—context and left the answer to the guests at the banquet. That is to say, he certainly did not advocate a *laissez-faire, laissez-aller* ideology. He equally refused to settle the concrete dispute *expressis verbis*. Instead, using a parable which stimulates imaginative obedience, he placed the whole dispute in the wider framework of forgiveness and left 'the moral of the story' to his listeners. Always presupposing that the attitude of Jesus is his model, this means that the bishop must answer the dispute of the participants in a parable which forces them to regard their arguments from a new angle and to reply to their questions themselves. So the bishop is no judge. He recalls those who are running away from each other to the common table and encourages hope even when no concrete solution has been found. This does not mean suggesting

[20] W. Simpfendörfer, *op. cit.*, pp. 175-6.

a compromise. He embodies openness towards others by a question and a parable."[21]

Do such bishops exist? Certainly. Only think of John XXIII. Did he not ask questions which were so simple and yet so exciting that they stirred Catholic and Protestant Churches alike? Think of the Baptist, Martin Luther King. Did he not represent an openness towards others, the limits of which transcended his own powers of imagination? Such bishops are heard whether they are officially in office or not; and official bishops remain unheard if they are not episcopal men.

In short, I seek criteria for reforming the Church in those places which succeed in inviting the various "other Churches" together with the traditional ones to the banquet, to a dialogue in search of truth, to the celebration of the *communio oppositorum*. The theses of the "Church for others" and the petty reforms of the traditional Churches remain sectarian if we fail to experience the banquet of the *communio oppositorum* as an ecclesiological vinculum and hence as a criterion for reform.

[21] W. Simpfendörfer, *op. cit.*, pp. 177–8.

Translated by Irene Marinoff

Andrew M. Greeley

A Social Science Model for the Consideration of Religious Apostasy

THE purpose of this article will be to propose an alternative model for the consideration of religious apostasy to the one that seems to be assumed by most theologians and is taken for granted in most references to "secularization" in the pages of *Concilium*.

The model proposed by the conventional wisdom, at least as I understand it, sees apostasy as the result of fairly conscious, rational decision, made because Christianity has lost its credibility either because it is not able to cope with the problems presented by empirical science or because it cannot respond adequately to Marxist social criticism and to Marxist or to non-Marxist demands for social reform. The appropriate response to apostasy, it is then argued, is for the Church to become "relevant"; it must cope with the challenge of empirical science, it must respond to Marxist criticism either by embracing such criticism or by developing a "political criticism" of its own, and it must be deeply involved in the work of social reform. In the words of Dietrich Bonhoffer, "Man has come of age," and the Church, too, must come of age by being empirical, critical and revolutionary.

It is certainly not the intention of the present writer to decry a concern for meaningful dialogue between Christianity and empirical science, although it is worth noting that at the present time the positive sciences have serious problems of their own. Nor would I wish at all to question the necessity for the clergy to become involved in social criticism and action, but I would want to insist that such involvement ought to be marked by much higher levels of professional competence than has hitherto been demonstrated by many enthusiastic critics and reformers. I simply want to contend that these activities cannot reasonably be expected to win back those who have "left the Church" or to prevent apostasy among those who are inclined to it. No matter how modern or relevant the Church is, it will not have much impact on apostasy rates *precisely because apostasy has relatively little to do with the actions of the Church.*

I have in other publications strongly questioned the simple evolutionary model which views man as moving from the sacred to the secular. I do not propose in the present article to repeat the argument beyond saying that only the most naïve theologian can at the present time persist in accepting such a model.[1] It is my purpose, rather, to raise the strong question as to whether apostasy represents a meaningful beginning point for devising religious strategy.

To the sociologist religion is man's "meaning system" or his "interpretive scheme"; that is to say, the set of answers to fundamental questions man asks about the nature and purpose of reality. It is, as Clifford Geertz noted, "the relatively modest assumption that God is not mad." Religion answers the question of whether reality is gracious or evil, whether the really real is accessible or inaccessible, how man harmonizes his own existence with the nature of reality, and how the good man ought to live.[2] This interpretive scheme or world-view underpins all the other human meaning systems, such as science, common sense, history, ideology. As Geertz points out, in the absence of responses to the fundamental questions, the universe loses its interpretability and all other meaning systems are called into question. Religion may be implicit and it may be called into play only when man is faced with death or mystery, or physical or moral evil, but the very fact that responses to the fundamental questions exist and can be called into use when they are required protects man from being overpowered by chaos.

[1] See, for example, the recent issue of *Social Research* (Summer, 1970) devoted to the question of "resacralization".

[2] It would not be appropriate in this article to develop at any great length the sociologist's assumption that religion is a "culture system". The interested reader might consult the writings of Clifford Geertz, especially *Islam Observed*, and Thomas Luckmann, especially *The Invisible Religion*.

The responses to the fundamental religious questions may not at all be positive; they may not postulate a sacred or a transcendent, though there is, apparently, a strong strain for man to sacralize his meaning system even if he denies the existence of a transcendental referent. Some men may have a greater need for an explicit and developed meaning system than others, but from the viewpoint of sociologists of religion, no one can do without it; hence, Emil Durkheim's phrase, "There will always be religion".

To a very considerable extent we inherit our interpretive scheme, or, to put the matter more precisely, we absorb it from the environment of our early childhood much the way we absorb our language. Since religion deals with the most ultimate of man's questions, it also necessarily deals with the most intimate of his self-definition and is shaped especially by the first intimate relationship he experiences—the triad of himself, his mother and his father. Religious socialization, then, is deeply affected, indeed, probably fundamentally shaped by a child's early interaction experiences with his parents and by the view of reality he absorbs from them during that interaction.

In his later life he may clarify, explore, reinforce and develop that interpretive scheme, or he may, in fact, turn away from it and reject it. However, it should be noted that it is not any easier to drastically change one's interpretive scheme in adult life than it is to change one's language; in fact, it is probably much more difficult. An adult who contends on the level of rational consciousness that he has left behind the religion of his parents is still likely in the subconscious and unconscious levels of his personality to be profoundly affected by that interpretive scheme.

The social scientist is inclined to hypothesize that religious apostasy will occur more frequently among those whose childhood experiences have been tense, difficult or troubled. One's religion is intimately identified with one's parents and one's early family. If nothing has happened to predispose a person to turn definitively away from his parents and his early family experiences, then it is very unlikely in the hypothesis that there will be much of a predisposition to reject one's childhood religion.

The research evidence in support of this hypothesis has been increasing rapidly in recent years. Josep Zelan discovered that religious apostasy among college graduates was most likely to

occur among those with tense, alienated and unhappy per-
sonalities. David Caplovitz, following up Zelan's research, showed
that such personality predispositions in religious apostates could
be linked with early family relationships. My own research on
Catholics who had graduated from college has suggested that the
predisposition of certain Catholics to leave the Church was already
present in their teenage years and had relatively little to do with
whether or not they attended a Catholic college.

John Kotre designed a research project to study specifically
religious apostasy among graduate students at two major American universities. The design of his study was such that all of his
hundred respondents were graduate students at secular universities
who had spent their grammar school, high school and college
years at Catholic schools. Half of them defined themselves as "in
the Church"; the other half defined themselves as "outside the
Church".

Kotre discovered that there were relatively few differences in
fundamental religious or moral attitudes between the two groups
but very considerable differences in their family backgrounds.
Those who defined themselves as "out" of the Church (most of
them men) tended to come from families where there was either
religious or personal conflict or both. Indeed, Kotre was able to
explain most of the variants between the "ins" and the "outs" in
terms of family background experience. He observed that whether
a graduate student defined himself as in the Church or out of the
Church depended in considerable measure on how he chose to
define the Church and that, in its turn, was a function of which
of the many stimuli the Church emits he chose to focus on. Kotre
commented that to a very considerable extent the stimuli one
focuses on is a function of one's own personality which is, of
course, shaped substantially by one's childhood experiences. Those
who were "out" of the Church perceived the Church differently
because their personality orientations were different from those
who defined themselves as "in".

In research in which I am currently involved with William
McCready, we have discovered that the two most powerful pre-
dictors of adult religious behaviour are the religious behaviour of
parents and the religious behaviour of one's spouse, and that the
influence of these variables will persist over three generations. We

conclude, therefore, that the fundamental religious orientation of an adult is shaped by his childhood experiences.

In research presently being done at the National Opinion Research Center on the American Catholic priesthood it was hypothesized that the theory of religious apostasy might be extended to include the question of resigning from the priesthood. It was suggested that there might be a positive correlation between tension in the family background and proclivity to leave the active priesthood. While the results of this project are not yet complete and precise statistics are not available for release at the present time, it is still quite safe to say that the hypothesis received considerable support from the data.

It is important to note that none of the research summarized in the previous paragraphs indicates an absolute identity between apostasy and tension in one's family background although Kotre does in his study manage to explain most of the variance between the "ins" and the "outs". Moreover, what is being asserted is that not all those who have tense family backgrounds apostatize, nor that all who are apostates come from tense family backgrounds. It is, rather, that those with tense family backgrounds are far more likely to be apostates than those from relatively pleasant family backgrounds.

It also should be noted that what one is considering in this research is a more or less permanent and definitive turning away from the religion of one's origin, not temporary periods of doubt, hesitancy or cessation of religious practice.

A good deal more research will of course be necessary to refine and develop this model of religious apostasy. However, even at the present time one is justified in saying that it has been established beyond all reasonable doubt that unconscious personality drives, deeply rooted in early childhood experiences, play an extremely important role in the decision of many people to turn away from the religious interpretive scheme they absorbed in childhood.

It will be perceived that this model calls into serious question the validity of the "secularization", "man comes of age" model. It is obvious that some advanced industrialized nations such as England, Scandinavia and France are areas of quite low religious practice and affiliation. It is also obvious that in certain other countries the Church has become identified with the forces opposing evolution or social reform. On the other hand, certain very advanced industrialized nations such as the United States, Canada and Holland have quite high levels of religious affiliation and practice; and in other nations, such as Ireland, the Church has traditionally been strongly affiliated with a revolutionary movement. Furthermore, the research of the British sociologist David Martin shows that while religious practice and affiliation may be relatively low in England, it does not necessarily follow that the British population is atheistic. Quite the contrary, even many of those who no longer can agree with the existence of God still endorse religious education in the schools. Furthermore, Martin notes that the so-called "de-christianization" of certain areas in England is not a recent phenomenon. For example, a survey of the diocese of St David in Wales in the early 1700's shows that the level of religious affiliation and practice was quite low even at that time.

The French religious geographers can trace the religious behaviour of certain segments of the French population to situations and events which occurred centuries ago. Still other writers suggest that the conversion of the Scandinavian countries to Christianity before the Reformation was a very superficial and tenuous affair and that Reformation piety itself never sunk very deep roots in Norway or Sweden.

When one views these data and the data on the psycho-dynamics of apostasy reported in the previous paragraphs, one begins to understand that apostasy is a highly complex issue. He who wishes to understand it must ask himself two questions: what is the interpretive scheme that a young person inherits from his society and his parents; and what is the process by which he absorbs the interpretive scheme?

The "religion" of a society as mediated through the parents to the child would be in the Western world a very complex mixture of pre-Christian paganism and superstition, Christianity (partly élite and partly folk), modern science, contemporary political ideology, and formulations more or less sophisticated of contemporary psychoanalysis, existentialism and Marxism (or, alternately, Capitalism). The precise blending of all these elements will depend both on the experience of a child's parents and on the experience of the larger society of which they are a part. And, indeed, the aspects of each element emphasized will also be a result of the family and societal experience. Thus, for reasons of politics and history, the Catholics of Ireland have put heavy emphasis on canonical requirements for church attendance, whereas Catholics in other cultures will stress those aspects of Catholicism which consider strict adherence for canonical regulations much less important than certain personality styles. To put the matter differently, frequent church attendance in Ireland is intimately connected with the fundamental view of the Irish Catholic on the nature of reality. However, for the Italian Catholic, let us say, the intimate relationship between appearing in church every Sunday and one's basic interpretive scheme is much less evident.

Thus, one can see that the de-christianization of a country like France is a result of a whole complex of social and historical phenomena by which frequent church attendance, explicit affiliation, and even self-definition as Christian became identified with certain social and political classes. Similarly, Martin explains the lack of influence of the Church of England on large segments of the working class as the result of the historical identification of the Anglican Church with the landed gentry. In other words, everything in the world-view of the son of a man in the British or French working class militates against close identification with Anglicanism in England and Catholicism in France. On the other hand, in Ireland (as probably in Poland also) explicit loyalty to and identification with Catholicism—and Catholicism in its most strict canonical forms—has been reinforced by the linkage between Irish nationalism and the Church. The biggest favour the British government ever did for the Irish Church was to define it as an enemy of British rule in Ireland.

Furthermore, in multi-denominational countries like the United States, Canada, Holland or Switzerland, the very fact of religious pluralism makes religion available as an important means of self-definition over against the other segments of society. High levels of church attendance in these countries are to be observed because religion and church attendance are essential to the self-definition of considerable numbers of people in a pluralistic society. However, in a "one Church" country or in a country where there is an "established" Church practically identified with the society, religion plays a much less important role in self-definition and levels of church attendance are apt to be considerably lower.

It may be argued, of course, that if the French Church had been able to escape the political and social identifications of the past, it would not have "lost" the working class. Surely such an observation is true, but it does not follow therefore that attempts to identify with the working class at the present time will be successful in winning them back to the Church (however appropriate and necessary such identification may be). From the earliest period of his life a French working-class child learns to be sceptical and suspicious of the official Church. Indeed, one might even say that such suspicion and scepticism is part of his religion, part of his basic world-view or interpretive scheme.

Society, history, culture, economics and politics help to shape the world-view which is available to a child. His own experience plays a considerable role in determining the extent to which he will extend his world-view in later life. The model being suggested here will become clear if we consider four different possibilities: an Irish Catholic with a relatively pleasant childhood experience, an Irish Catholic with a tense and painful childhood experience, a French Communist with a relatively pleasant childhood experience and a French Communist with a tense and painful childhood experience.

The model being presented here in this paper would suggest that there will be a high probability (though not a certainty) that the first person will remain a Catholic, going to church every Sunday throughout his whole life. There will also be some considerable likelihood that person *b* will disaffiliate himself in one way or another from church practice or from the Church itself. Person *c* is likely to remain a devout and sincere Communist all his life, though perhaps he will flirt temporarily with Maoism during his years in university. Person *d* is likely, on the other hand, to "apostatize" from orthodox Communism, either by moving to the "left" and becoming a Maoist or by moving to the "right" and becoming a Christian.

One does not wish to deny either that freedom of choice about one's religious posture can be exercised by an adult or that Marxism, logical positivism and existentialism may play some sort of role in a conscious rational decision about religious faith and ecclesiastical affiliation. One does want to assert that such conscious rational decisions quite free from the psychodynamics acquired in childhood are not nearly as frequent as the conventional model of apostasy assumes. On the contrary, one may even assert that such decisions are probably relatively infrequent.

One may hazard a perhaps unpopular conclusion for theologians and religious leaderships. "De-christianization" and "apostasy" are complex, subtle and extremely difficult phenomena. They involve enormously powerful social, psychological, historical and cultural forces. These forces will not be overcome by quick adaptation of structures, by facile reformulations of message, or by shallow attempts to obtain "instant relevance" or instant skills at social and political criticism. The "diaspora"—understood as a very low level of identification with the organized Christian Church—has not come into being overnight and will not be exorcized easily. The work of Martin and others helps us to realize that those in the diaspora may not in fact be any less Christian in their most fundamental view of the nature of reality than were their ancestors. It hardly need be observed that even those who are most consciously and explicitly affiliated with a Church frequently include within their world-view substantial segments of paganism, be it the superstitious paganism of the past or the scientific paganism of the present.

Both fundamental world-view and ecclesiastical affiliation, then, are the result of the interweaving of very complex social forces. The religious situation in a given person or in a given society admits of no easy explanations and surely of no simple and facile solutions. The "apostasy" of either an individual or a society is not likely to be changed quickly or easily and, alas, in most circumstances, short of overwhelming amounts of divine grace, not at all.

Of course, the Church must try, if only because that is the mission on which it has been sent, and also because its own blunders and mistakes of the past have contributed greatly to the many sad situations of the present. But in terms of economy of effort the Church must also understand that its most plausible payoff in terms of the humanization and christianization of the world is going to come from efforts to strengthen and deepen and enrich the faith of those who are already explicitly and consciously members of the household of the faith and who are not angry at that household because it has become identified with a home in which they grew up. Again, let me say that I am not suggesting that apostates are to be abandoned. I am saying that while one must always have hope in God's grace, in the ordinary course of human events one cannot expect one's efforts in this area to be very successful.

PART III
DOCUMENTATION
CONCILIUM

Bärbel Kopetzky

The End of Church-building and the Start of Building up the Church?

A FEW weeks ago what is known as "Church-building Sunday" was celebrated in the Netherlands. On this Sunday every year money is collected in all churches for new church buildings. As usual, Cardinal Alfrink gave a suitable address, in which, how-ever, the aim of the spending was considerably modified. In his view, one could no longer speak of a "Church-building Sunday"; it would be better to talk of a "Sunday for Building up the Church".[1] In the present stage of development of the Dutch Church, he said, it was no longer appropriate to spend the money exclusively on church buildings. In the pastoral field, investments in men and materials were far more pressing and desirable. The Church could no longer keep pace with the expansion of the towns and erect churches in the new residential districts; it should strive primarily to provide the best possible pastoral care of people, and that meant renouncing representative public buildings.

This allocution of Cardinal Alfrink's shows clearly that today we are at a turning-point in church-building. To this example could be added similar events in other countries and Churches: for example, the protest against excessively ostentatious cathedrals in the United States or the decision made by the Evangelical Lutheran community of Harburg (Germany) in 1970 to provide no further resources for new church buildings.[2] Obviously, in wide

[1] Cf. T. Claessens, "Kerkcenten", *De Bazuin,* 7 March 1971, pp. 6-7.
[2] Friedrich Gleiss, "Lieber etwas bescheidener planen. Müssen weiterhin neue Kirchen gebaut werden?", *Luth. Monatshefte,* 9 (1970), pp. 508-11.

circles inside and outside the Church, church-building has ceased to seem self-evidently desirable.

This development has long been heralded in a number of different publications on the subject of church-building. Theologians and architects have been trying since about 1960 to conduct a critical analysis of the vast amount of church-building that went on after 1945—probably never before have so many churches been built as in the two decades after 1945. One of the first critical voices was raised at the Eucharistic Congress in Munich in 1958, when R. Grosche delivered his "Reflections on the Theology of Church-building".[3] Since then a growing unease about traditional church-building (even in its modern wrapping) has made itself felt in many articles and at a number of Congresses. Criticism of traditional church-building is expressed on various different levels: from the angle of the liturgy, from the architectural and artistic standpoint, and in connection with pastoral-sociological and town planning considerations. It all firmly ends in the question, is it really possible and permissible to go on building churches?[4]

In the following survey we shall try, with the help of the literature, to show what the present tendencies and problems of church-building are; and we shall do this in an historical context, from the cathedrals of the Gothic revival to the "Stadthalle Monheim".[5] As a preliminary, the problem of the antithesis "sacred-profane" will be briefly discussed in connection with church-building; and in conclusion an attempt will be made to relate the changes in church-building to those in ecclesiology. This will justify, I hope, the appearance of this survey in an issue devoted to ecclesiology.

I. The Holy, the Sacred and the Profane

It is naturally impossible within the confines of a survey like this to give a detailed exposition of learned discussion of the holy and the sacred. This would mean pushing deep into the realms of

[3] In *"Et extra et intra"*, *Theol. Aufsätze* (Düsseldorf, 1958), pp. 99–106.
[4] Cf. the "Stadthalle Monheim" project by W. M. Förderer in G. Rombold (ed.), *Kirchen für die Zukunft bauen* (Vienna and Freiburg, 1969), pp. 162 f.
[5] Cf. W. Weyres, "Können wir noch Kirchenbauen?", *Hochland*, 60 (1968), pp. 644–54.

the history of religion and philosophy, of aesthetics and theology,[6] and expounding the problem in all its breadth. We shall therefore restrict ourselves to a few remarks sketching the background to the whole problem of church-building.

Let us begin by considering what is known as "desacralization" or "desanctification"; here opinions differ considerably. In France,[7] for example, J. Daniélou demands the renewed sanctification of sections of the world, a "Christian milieu", to support the Christian faith of the masses. "In a world threatened by atheism", he says, "the substance of the sacred must be defended wherever it is present."[8] A quite different view is held by M-D. Chenu,[9] who greets the desanctification of society with enthusiasm and sees it as a possible way to a purer Christianity. According to Chenu, one can recognize in the progress of our world in the realm of humanization, socialization and so forth a kind of "*praeparatio evangelica*".

It would be possible to mention many other names in connection with "desacralization", but this would not affect the position. On the one side we have conservative theologians, who want a Christianity anchored in a sacral culture or civilization to protect the simple faith of ordinary people, and on the other progressive theologians who see in the desacralization of society, the secularization of the world and the de-institutionalization of the Church a liberation of the Church in the spirit of the Gospel. One could almost speak here of a need on the part of Catholic theology to catch up on worldliness. The debate with the modern world, continually interrupted since the nineteenth century, has been developing quickly with Vatican II. The dialogue with the other Christian Churches leads to the Church's moving further from its own past and to the swift adoption of the idea of secularization. On the whole, people are sceptical of the notion of the

[6] For bibliography cf. E. Syndicus, "Entsakralisierung. Ein Literaturbericht", *Theologie u. Phil.*, 42 (1967), pp. 577–90; E. J. Lengeling, "Sakral—profan, Bericht über die gegenwärtige Diskussion", *Liturgisches Jahrbuch*, 18 (1968), pp. 164–88.

[7] On the French discussion cf. C. Geffré, "The Tension between Desacralization and Spirituality", *Concilium*, 9, 2 (Nov. 1966), pp. 57–66 (American edn., vol. 19).

[8] J. Daniélou, *L'Oraison problème politique* (Paris, 1965), p. 98.

[9] M.-D. Chenu, *La Parole de Dieu II, L'Evangile dans le temps* (Paris, 1964). Cf. Geffré, *op. cit.*, pp. 57–8.

"sacred", even to the point of feeling an aversion for it. H. Christoffe himself speaks of a "diabolical transformation of faith into things",[10] and thinks that this deals once and for all with the problem of the holy. But most theologians prefer to emphasize the independence and worldliness of the world and to speak at the same time of a consecration of the world. It is not entirely clear in what relationship these two pronouncements stand to each other.

This approach finds its logical extension in the arguments about religious art, a concept which is increasingly rejected. K. Ledergerber[11] expounds the contrast between the New Testament and the later practice of the Catholic Church in regard to the sacred. Christ spiritualized the religious inheritance of his people; but this work of spiritualization was gradually undone by the Church, which once again allowed the sacred to make itself at home in the Church and thereby slipped back into a pre-Christian attitude. The dimension of holiness is illegitimate in the context of the New Testament.[12]

In 1967 Walter Warnack once again made the attempt to establish the criteria for a sacred art. The stages he defined were these: (1) the moment of negativity, (2) the moment of the wound, the parting, and (3) the moment of duality.[13] Aber J. Hennig points out in the very same collection of essays that these criteria are not related at all to the essential aim of sacred art, but to a temporally and geographically limited conception of it which is "the expression of a Teutonic view of life".[14]

To turn to church-building, what does sacredness mean here? P. Antoine adopts the criteria of Mircea Eliade:[15] (1) the holy

[10] H. Christoffels, "Die Religion zwischen Argwohn und Glaube", in *Baumer, Christoffels, Mainberger, Das Heilige in Licht und Zwielicht* (Einsiedeln, 1966), quoted in Syndicus, *op. cit.*, p. 580.
[11] K. Ledergerber, *Kunst und Religion in der Verwandlung* (Cologne, 1961).
[12] Th. Sartory, "Entgrenzung des Sakralen", in *Eine Neuinterpretation des Glauben* (Einsiedeln, 1966), pp. 82–107.
[13] W. Warnach, "Sakrale Kunst?", in *Das Sakrale im Widerspruch*, ed. by T. Bogler, *Laacher Hefte 41* (Maria Laach, 1967), pp. 84 ff.
[14] J. Hennig, "Einige Gedanken zu den Ausführungen von W. Warnach", *op. cit.*, pp. 97–9.
[15] P. Antoine, "L'Eglise est-elle un lieu sacré?", *Etudes* (1967), pp. 432–47, reprinted in the omnibus volume: P. Antoine and E. Martin, *La quérelle*

(*sacré*) place is clearly divided from the profane place; (2) the holy place is not chosen arbitrarily, but is originally connected with a hierophany (repetition of the myth of creation at the consecration ceremony), and (3) the structure of the holy place is modelled on that of the world (p. 585). Antoine shows that medieval churches display these essential features: the church with its tower forms the axis of the world; it is the geographical centre of the town; and the rite of consecration brings to life the redemption of the world in the representation of Christ's victory over Satan. Thus in the Middle Ages there was a unique link between church and sacred place. The church reflected the social order and sanctioned it. But the old total view of the world has been destroyed by modern technology. In a technological world there are no longer any holy places, for even the holy mount can be altered by technology (p. 586). The holy is now linked to human relations: Lourdes is holy because of the people who pray there (p. 587).

These arguments are complemented by C. Werner's[16] penetrating analysis of the way in which the word "sacred" is used in modern times. Our modern understanding of "sacred" is rooted in Romanticism, when the consciousness of history awakes. On "artistic excursions"[17] people discover the aesthetic as a realm of its own. The spirit of the Middle Ages is sought in its churches, because this spirit makes you feel pious; here people wanted to share in the sphere of the religious, the sacred. "The sacred becomes a matter of atmosphere" (p. 69). To guarantee this atmosphere, nineteenth-century church-building took up the Gothic style again, and modern church architecture also tries to evoke this impression by employing archaic elements.

In the last few years, however, new ideas about the holy and the sacred have made their appearance. In contrast to the situation

---

du sacré (Paris, 1970). (Série: Verse et controverse.) [The quotations in the text are taken from the Dutch translation of the essay "Is een kerk een sacrale plaats?", *Streven*, 20 (1966–7), pp. 584–94.]

[16] Christof Werner, "Sakralität—was ist das?", in *Kirchen in nachsakraler Zeit*, ed. by H.-E. Bahr, *Konkretionen 3* (Hamburg, 1968), pp. 64–80.

[17] The first excursion of this sort was the trip made by L. Tieck and W. Wackenroder through Franconia in 1793. The literary result of this journey was "Die Herzensergiessungen eines kunstliebenden Klosterbruders", 1797, cf. C. Werner, *op. cit.*, p. 65.

prevailing in magic and nature religions, says Jacques Grand'-Maison,[18] the sacred is not something existing in its own right, but a relationship. According to J. Splett,[19] however, all sacredness as a relationship has its basis and origin in the *holy*. The Christian message has certainly eliminated the difference between the sacred and the real world, but the world remains ambiguous. In the symbol, in the sacrament of the Eucharist, we encounter the holy, i.e., the person Jesus Christ.

The New Testament scholar H. Schürmann[20] also tries to speak in subtler terms than before of the "desacralization" of religion introduced by Jesus. In the Christian revelation, he says, the naturally sacred element is "eschatologized", "preumatized" and finally "christologized". In spite of this, the presence of the Lord needs a mediatory symbol: his presence shines out in the eschatological festivity[21] of the community.

II. REDISCOVERY OF HISTORICISM

Who has never had the experience of entering a neo-Gothic church and being repelled by it? The dark, cramping space, the uncomfortable pews, the absence of style and the mustiness are all alien to our modern attitude to life. Yet these churches were once modern and breathed a new spirit! For a long time people paid no attention to this style of building and more or less dismissed it from their minds.[22] It is only recently that the ecclesiastical architecture of the nineteenth century has come under discussion.

It will perhaps be easier for us to understand this period if we recall that the *Liturgical Movement* rose at the same time and

[18] J. Grand'Maison, *Le Monde et le Sacré. I. Le Sacré* (Paris, 1966), pp. 25, 58, 80.
[19] J. Splett, *Sakrament der Wirklichkeit. Vorüberlegungen zu einem weltlichen Begriff des Heiligen* (Würzburg, 1968), pp. 87 ff.
[20] H. Schürmann, "Neutestamentliche Marginalien zur Frage der 'Entsakralisierung' ", *Der Seelsorger*, 38 (1968), pp. 38–48, 89–104.
[21] The meaning of the festival for the Christian community and for man in general is being rediscovered today: cf. Josef Pieper, *Zustimmung zur Welt. Eine Theorie des Festes* (Munich, 1963); H. Fortmann, *Hoogtijd, gedachten over feesten en vasten* (Baarn, 1970²); H. Cox, *Feast of Fools* (1970).
[22] Compare, for example, the very short and disparaging remarks on Historicism in the articles "Kirchenbau" in the *Lexikon für Theol. und Kirche²* and in *"Religion in Gesch. und Gegenwart"³*.

that the new style of building was propagated by the same ecclesiastical (and revitalizing) forces that produced the renewal of the liturgy. In general, it is not too difficult for us to pass a positive verdict on the Liturgical Movement. We can likewise recognize an uninterrupted continuation of the Liturgical Movement in the twentieth century. With the help of C. Werner's article,[23] we have already emphasized in the previous section the connection between our time and the nineteenth century in its aesthetic judgments: the idea was to create, with the assistance of the Gothic style, a sacred space. But this view of neo-Gothic churches is too one-sided; other standpoints must be taken into consideration if we want to gain an accurate picture of the situation.

The fact is that the "historical" style had been on the advance since the forties of the last century. It was widely employed all over Europe and North America, and even in the mission countries. No Christian Church escaped its embrace and it was soon prescribed wherever architects were commissioned to build new churches.[24] As late as 1912 a decree issued by the Archdiocese of Cologne required the "Romanesque, Gothic or what is known as the transitional style" for church-building![25] Through the enormous increase and urbanization of the population as a result of industrialization there was a great deficiency of churches, which was made good by the wholesale erection of neo-Gothic ones.

Since unfortunately too little historical material has so far been sifted, it will be permissible, I think, to adduce an example from the Anglican Church. In a short essay B. F. L. Clarke has investigated the ideals of the "Ecclesiologists".[26] The "Ecclesiological Society", founded in 1839 in Oxford and reorganized in 1844 in London, with many branches throughout England, was an association of architects—most of them young—and theologians. They were in search of the right architectural style for

[23] See note 16.
[24] E.g., in the Evangelical Churches of Germany: the Regulations for the construction of Evangelical churches at Eisenach 1861, somewhat toned down in the Eisenach Counsels of 1898.
[25] Cf. article "Kirchenbau V." by H. Hampe in RGG III³ (1959), Sp. 1395.
[26] Basil F. L. Clarke, "The Ideals of the Ecclesiologists", Theology, 73 (1970), pp. 351–9.

churches and wanted so far as possible to use it in practice. Their choice of the Gothic style was inspired (at any rate in the first place) not by romantic feeling or archaeological enthusiasm but by their conviction that this style was the only true Christian one uncontaminated by any pagan influences (p. 354). Gothic adornments of the sort usual at the end of the eighteenth century and the beginning of the nineteenth were rejected. They wanted to arrive at a constructive Gothic style and to avoid the utilitarianism of their predecessors. The aim was to design a building suited to its purpose, and by purpose was understood the celebration of the sacraments, the gathering of the community, the reading from Scripture, the sermon, and morning and evening prayers. For this reason the altar was placed at the central point, the font was given a good position and special pews for certain families were abolished. The church was to provide room for all. This kind of church gave rise to an "ecclesiastical" mode of thought: these churches were intended to provide solid evidence of the presence of the Christian faith in a world filled with ideas of progress. The contrast with the world was underlined and an attempt was made by means of ancient symbols (e.g., the orientation of the church) to preserve the supernatural element and make it something that could be felt.

H. Mai's thesis[27] also produces a more finely shaded picture of church-building in the nineteenth century. He examined church buildings in the territory of the present East German state, and demonstrates in detail the connections between the renewal of the liturgy and church-building; he also points to the adoption of the idea of the symbol from Romanticism (ground-plan and so forth) and the decoration of churches with a view to the production of a total impression. In addition, he puts church-building in its cultural and sociological context. "A particularly important result of my investigations", he says, "is their proof of the incorrectness of the widespread opinion that church-building in the 'historical' style is a sign of a spiritually dead and socially barren Church" (p. 792). In Mai's view, these churches, too, deserve to be protected

---

[27] H. Mai, *Studien zum Kirchenbau des 19. Jahrhunderts* (Leipzig, 1970) (in typescript), summary in *Theol. Literaturzeitung*, 95 (1970), pp. 791-3.

as historical monuments, because they represent a unique phenomenon. "One can understand (this kind of ecclesiastical architecture) as an effort, conditioned by the period, to bear convincing
Christian witness in a post-Enlightenment age" (p. 793).

III. REVIVAL OF CHURCH ARCHITECTURE

Only gradually has the predominance of "historicism" in
church-building been broken in the twentieth century. Apparently
people had grown too well accustomed to this style and identified
it with church buildings in general. Nevertheless, the opening
years of this century produced a few buildings that still look
modern today. The first architect[28] to be named must be the
American, Frank Lloyd Wright. In 1906 he built the Unitarian
church at Oak Park (Chicago) in prefabricated concrete. The
building is distinguished by its structural honesty; anything purely
decorative was omitted. On the side facing the street the church
is linked to the adjoining school, and in its style does not stand
out from its surroundings. The monumental style is typical of
Wright's normal mode of building, which is on the whole always
monumental. The interior of the building is clearly structured and
attempts to integrate the congregation in groups. Unfortunately
the construction of the inside does not allow any spontaneous
grouping.

For Europe, A. Perret's Notre Dame du Raincy (Paris, 1922)
was a milestone in the development of church architecture. For
the creation of this edifice the Church is indebted more to lack of
money on the part of those who commissioned it than to their
modern views. Perret was concerned to show in this building that
reinforced concrete could be used for anything. The plan of the
church is by no means revolutionary: it is a basilica of nave and
aisles. What is special about it is its proportions: it is a high, open
space with hardly any refinements of styling and devoid of any
kind of sentimentality. This church forms an invitation to life and

---

[28] For what follows, use has been made of *RGG* and *LThK* (Article
Kirchenbau) und G. Bekaert, *In een of ander huis, kerkbouw op een
keerpunt* (Tielt-den Haag, 1968), which contains many pictures and detailed
descriptions of buildings illustrating the development of modern church
architecture.

the liturgy. The tower section forms something of a contradiction to the rest; it seeks a way out in the monumental.

The third modern church we should like to mention is the church of the Restored Apostolic Community in the Kiefhoek district of Rotterdam (1929). Its architect, J. J. P. Oud, had looked himself for an ecclesiastical organization to take over his church. He had designed the church in the context of his plan for the district as a whole. The church lies on the edge of the district and is stylistically adapted to it. There can be talk here of domination of the surroundings. The severe lines of the building correspond to those of the blocks of flats. This church leaves an impression of habitability, in contrast to the many massive "low level" churches of those years.

IV. THE LITURGY AS ARCHITECT

The revival of church architecture in Germany has pursued a rather different course from the one exemplified in the buildings so far mentioned. Here the impetus came mainly from the Liturgical Movement and not so much from architecture. Otto Bartning, Dominikus Böhm and Rudolf Schwarz were all close to this movement, which developed on both the Catholic and Evangelical sides out of the youth movement. They seek a form from the liturgical events; indeed, the architectural form itself takes part in the liturgy. There are experiments with new materials; an example of this is Bartning's steel church at the Press Exhibition in Cologne in 1928. There is an attempt in form and plan to create a sacred space or enclosure. In his "Star Church" (1922; only a design) Bartning employs a cosmic symbol. Rudolf Schwarz's magnificent Corpus Christi church (Aachen, 1928) is a tall cube, the bare walls of which point forward and upward. The effect produced by this church is breathtaking; it is impossible to look away from the central happening on the altar. The individual is overcome by a feeling of the pettiness of his existence; here he encounters a quite different world. Also worth mentioning are the churches of D. Böhm, who has had many imitators. Here we find, instead of the severity of Schwarz's churches, a positively Baroque wealth of forms (e.g. St Engelbert, Riehl, Cologne, 1930). The many round-headed arches produce a strong effect:

"We have the definite feeling that we are entering an ecstatic space—the profane is left behind us".[29]

To sum up, it must be said that we are faced here with monumental buildings which—standing out from their surroundings—point with their cosmic and archaic forms to a sacred world order. The relationship to the "historical" kind of church interior is certainly clear enough.

V. Mass-produced Churches

After 1945 came an epoch of church-building of unknown dimensions. In Germany alone in a period of twenty years some six thousand new churches were erected, two thousand each for the Catholic Church, the Evangelical Church and the Free Churches.[30] In the Netherlands it is reckoned that up to 1963 about thirteen hundred new churches were built; in France six thousand new churches have been constructed since 1918. In other European countries the figures are lower, but even in these countries there has been an astonishing amount of activity in the field of building.[31]

Immediately after the Second World War emergency churches were put up to provide temporary replacements for the many churches in ruins and to offer some kind of focus for the thousands of homeless. They are modest buildings without any claim to distinction, often built in the shape of a tent out of prefabricated sections. After the war, Bartning, Böhm and Schwarz soon resumed their activities, which had been interrupted by the Third Reich. Once again they gave expression to the idea of a sacred space, but with Schwarz[32] it is possible to note a further development towards the simple vessel enclosing space, a vessel which also stands out less in outward form from its surroundings.

There is little point in citing here as many examples as possible of modern church architecture. Each of us will be familiar with a certain number from his own experience. What strikes one about most churches is the imposing nature of the forms employed.

[29] G. Bekaert, op. cit., p. 63.
[30] F. Gleiss, loc. cit., p. 508.   [31] G. Bekaert, op. cit., p. 13.
[32] Cf. G. Bekaert, "Rudolf Schwarz. Desacralisatie van het kerkgebouw", Streven (1962), pp. 645-51.

One almost has the impression that architects make use of church-building as an opportunity to give their imagination free play and to demonstrate their artistic gifts. But obviously the Christian Churches, too, need to present themselves to the public in modern, or to be more accurate, modernistic buildings and thus to assert their position as leaders of culture.

In contrast to the situation prevailing in the past, even architects with big reputations participate in church-building. World-famous examples of this are Le Corbusier's Pilgrimage Chapel at Ronchamp (1954) or his Dominican monastery of La Tourette near Lyons (1960), Mies van der Rohe's chapel for the Illinois Institute of Technology in Chicago (1952), and Aalto's Vuoksen-niska church at Imatra (1958). Many other examples could be quoted, but this would make little difference to the conclusion. The churches designed by great architects do not testify to a new conception of the Church; they repeat traditional ideas with the help of the new architecture.

Less well known architects try to imitate the famous ones and design tremendously expressive churches which then form a strong contrast to the monotonous and wearisome new urban districts. The result is often a deliberate modernity.

In conclusion, one positive aspect of modern church-building should be mentioned: the differences between Catholic and Reformed fashions are becoming smaller and smaller. Protestant church architecture, e.g., in the Netherlands,[33] has found a new relationship to forms and symbols. The communion table, the pulpit and the font acquire an importance of their own and are related to each other architecturally. And, vice versa, Catholic churches are losing their pictures, banners and other adornments; interior decoration is confined to the bare minimum.

VI. Criticism of Modern Church Architecture

The clearest statement is probably the one made by the empty seats in many new churches. Already many a local council has discovered that after the construction of the new church far fewer

[33] Cf. H. R. Blankesteijn, W. G. Overbosch, *Een hut om in te schuilen. Kerken van nu en morgen* (Baarn), who provide in this little book a survey of the best new Reformed churches in Holland.

people come to the services than came when they were held in a temporary hut or barn. The congregation does not feel at home in the ultra-modern building, whereas in the emergency church a real community came into existence spontaneously. The sterility and arbitrary nature of the forms awakens only distaste; quite a few of these churches are popularly known as "soul-silos". Are we confronted here merely with a certain cultural backwardness on the part of the faithful, which can be overcome, or is this a valid reaction?

Let us cite O. Graf's criticism: "We know very well that this Church founded to save souls builds many and big churches, but these buildings are a continual attempt to disguise death, to disguise the spiritual inability to seek new forms of organization and leave no stone unturned to find a way out of dead ends".[34]

The situation is certainly not as negative as Graf paints it. For several years people have been striving to clarify the question of church architecture. A particularly important event in this field was the architectural congress in New York in 1967.[35] Here a thorough investigation of the role of an institutionalized church in present-day society was demanded. The feeling that there was a pressing need for a change was strengthened by the group discussions. One of the most important speakers at this congress was F. Debuyst, who in his address rejected the monumental church architecture of modern times and with it the churches designed by famous architects. He expressed a preference for small, unassuming buildings—university chapels, among other things. In his view these modest buildings are much more appropriate to Christianity[36] because they take up again the tradition of the original Christian household. This house should be simple, hospitable and inconspicuous. The "holy" comes to pass there in the personal presence of the community. What is needed is an interior for the celebration of the Eucharist, whose "image" should be peace and *caritas* (p. 115). In this room a living community should

---

[34] Otto A. Graf, "Die Flucht in den Kirchenbau", *Hochland*, 61 (1969), pp. 266–72; here 268.

[35] Record of the congress: "Revolution, Place and Symbol", *Journal of the First International Congress on Religion, Architecture and the Visual Arts* (New York, 1969).

[36] F. Debuyst, "Anonyme Kirchen", *Wort und Wahrheit*, 24 (1969), pp. 113–8.

be able to develop; therefore nothing in the room should be permanently fixed. To Debuyst the ideal is the small household; at the parish level he reckons only on rooms for 200–400 people, for with larger numbers any personal encounter becomes impossible; J. M. Champlin, too, prefers a small church for socio-psychological reasons, but he also attaches importance to the possibilities of the new media and to experiments with a new liturgy.[37]

H. Schade[38] is committed to a completely different view. He thinks that the future of church architecture lies in a revival of the symbolic building, and refers to the Viennese painter Ernst Fuchs, who ventured to speak in his *"Architectura caelestis"* of a new temple. The horizontal nature of the consumer society is to be overcome by means of cosmic symbols (p. 124). Fundamentally, the article breathes distaste for modern technology and the social sciences. It is dubious whether the problems of the Church in modern society can be solved by this relapse into Romanticism and near-Fascist ideology.[39]

G. Rombold[40] traces the crisis in church architecture back to the crisis in the Church. Since Vatican II the Church wants to be a Church of dialogue and encounter. According to Rombold, it follows that church architecture must in future satisfy the following requirements: a church must no longer be a sacred building; instead of being a representational building it should be an inviting one, simple and plain from both the artistic and technical points of view. Moreover, this building should mirror the true position of the Church in society. The interior should be distinguished by qualities likely to develop a good sense of community and should also provide freedom for various different activities (pp. 162–5). In this connection, Rombold points out that

[37] J. M. Champlin, "Church Architecture in the Space Age", *The American Ecclesiastical Review*, CLX (1969), pp. 170–8.

[38] H. Schade, "Ende des Kirchenbaus", *Stimmen der Zeit*, 95 (Aug., 1970), pp. 117–24.

[39] Compare, for example, the arguments of Jörn Janssen, "Mythus des 20. Jahrhunderts in der Architekturtheorie", *Wort und Wahrheit*, 23 (1968), pp. 326–39.

[40] G. Rombold, "Kirchen für die Zukunft bauen", *Hochland*, 61 (1969), pp. 160–9, reprinted in the volume *Kirchen für die Zukunft bauen, loc. cit.*, pp. 201–17.

J. G. Davies[41] has proved the historical inaccuracy of the thesis of "the Liturgy as Architect". Up to the eighteenth century the church had all kinds of functions in the community, including that of providing the scene for such secular activities as Council Meetings, legal trials, school-teaching and wedding feasts. Rombold himself favours this manifold utilization of the church space. The duality of church and parish hall should disappear; in their place there should be a pastoral centre with bigger and smaller rooms.

Rombold's final reflections correspond to the demands of modern pastoral theologians,[42] who are striving for a re-structuring of the Christian community. They would like a parish centre which can act as a "service station". They also talk of various different community structures: functional communities (e.g., student communities) and parochial ones; household communities in a block of flats, and so on. All these forms only become possible if one ceases to regard the big parish church as the norm for church buildings.

Modern ecclesiastical architecture is also criticized from the sociological and town-planning angles. Churches are still conceived, so it is said, too much on the assumption of the people's church, which at bottom no longer exists in large areas of Europe.[43] Moreover, in the construction of a church more account should be taken of town-planning, so that the church can contribute to the integration of a new residential quarter.[44]

Also of some interest, perhaps, is the criticism of W. M. Förderer,[45] who attributes the failure of ecclesiastical architecture to an obsolete building programme. The nineteenth century has

[41] J. G. Davies, *The Secular Use of Church Buildings* (London, 1968).

[42] Cf. N. Greinacher, "Strukturwandel der Kirche heute und morgen", in *Kirchen für die Zukunft bauen . . .* , pp. 27-45.

[43] Cf. E. Bodzenta, "Gesellschaft und christliche Gemeinde", in *Kirchen für die Zukunft bauen*, pp. 9-25, and his contribution to the discussion in *Kirchenbau der Gegenwart* (Neudorfer Gespräche, 1968), *Tradition und Moderne Gesellschaft* I (Graz, 1969), pp. 64-9.

[44] Cf. H. Widtmann, "Pastorale, soziologische und städtebauliche Probleme des Kirchenbaues", in *Kirchen für die Zukunft bauen*, pp. 47-68, and his excellent introduction to the anthology, *Kirchenbau der Gegenwart*, loc. cit.

[45] W. M. Förderer, "Zentren politischer Urbanität", in *Kirchen in nachsakraler Zeit*, pp. 114-31.

dictated, down to today, what sort of things should be built: churches, schools, museums, theatres, dwelling-houses and town-halls. It is time for a change of approach. If we really want to liberate ourselves from historicism and Romanticism, then we must re-think the whole subject of ecclesiastical architecture; according to Förderer the result will be not modern *church-buildings*, but "simply *buildings for the Church* inspired by the needs of our age".[46]

VII. HUMANIZATION OF ARCHITECTURE: A HOUSE IN THE CITY OF MEN

The new programme for the presence of the Church in the city can probably best be indicated in the words of Cardinal Lercaro: "That the city of tomorrow, a not very distant tomorrow, should give itself a space for the meeting with the Lord, a space in which all men can gather round the one table and the one Word. A space that is firm and flexible, articulated in some way or other and built somewhere or other, but above all recognizable as a holy spot, not only because of the holy sacrifice that is offered there, but by virtue of the holiness of those who gather there."[47]

A few churches do exist in which something of this aim is achieved. The church of San Giovanni Battista on the motorway near Florence, built by G. Michelucci in 1964,[48] possesses an interior of human proportions. It conceals innumerable surprises; one feels at first as if one could never tire of looking round it. It is a considerable challenge to people to celebrate the liturgy here. Every kind of movement is allowed in the interior: sitting, standing, walking, running, dancing—it would be an ideal place for liturgical experiments, but unfortunately these have not yet taken place.

M. Dessauvage's[49] churches in Belgium are much more modest.

[46] W. M. Förderer, "Kirchenbau—Hindernis für den kirchlichen Auftrag?", in *Kirchen für die Zukunft bauen*, 156, pp. 149–65.
[47] Cardinal G. Lercaro, "Die Kirche in der Stadt von morgen", *Lit. Jahrbuch XVIII* (1968) (129–), p. 137.
[48] Cf. H. Schwebel, "In Aktion halten. Zur Kategorie des Menschlichen im Kirchenbau", *Kirchen in nachsakraler Zeit*, pp. 81–94, and G. Bekaert, *op. cit.*, pp. 89 f.
[49] *Idem*, pp. 98–100, 110.

These churches are ordinary houses without any allusion to the religious tradition in architecture. Dessauvage treats them like any other commission. He has succeeded in adapting his modern design to any kind of surroundings and thus in integrating old and new houses. His churches are distinguished by their habitability, simplicity and humanity; good examples are St Joseph's at Willebroek near Antwerp (1962), the village church of Ezemaal near Tienen (1965) and the college of St Lieven at Ghent (1965).

The third architect we should like to name here is W. M. Förderer,[50] whose most recent churches aim at integrating the Church in the social life of society. The Catholic parish church at Hérémence (Switzerland) forms part of his plan for the village. The bank, the shopping centre and a cafeteria form, together with the church, a massive complex. The interior of the church is so arranged that it can be used by the community for other purposes than church services—for theatrical performances, concerts and so forth. Another example is his design for the "Stadthalle Monheim". This is planned as a meeting-place for the citizens of the town and is intended to be seen as a service by the Church to society. A big hall is surrounded by smaller rooms: a kindergarten, a room for confirmation candidates, a room for young people, a room for old people, an office and a flat. The hall can be used for plays and concerts, ball games and the Sunday church service. The beginnings of a more human architecture and of true church-building in our age are adequately indicated in these examples. To these possibilities could also be added the idea of a church room in a block of flats or an office building.[51] The next few years will show whether further progress will be made along this path.

VIII. CHURCH-BUILDING AND ECCLESIOLOGY

In this final section I should like to venture on the attempt

[50] Cf. *Tradition und moderne Gesellschaft*, I, plate 10; *Kirchen für die Zukunft bauen*, pp. 162 f.

[51] Cf. the four kinds of future churches which P. Poscharsky, *Ende des Kirchenbaus?* (Stuttgart, 1969), foresees: the house church, the central church, the multi-purpose building and the building for worship.

to relate church-building and ecclesiology to one another. Ecclesiology is the theological doctrine of the Church, both visible and invisible. It is an effort to grasp and expound *hic et nunc* the institutional aspect of the Church and that of the company of the faithful. The community that gathers round the Word and the sacrament calls itself a Church, but this is also the term for the place where they gather. This "church building" is not a purely haphazard one; its shape is influenced by the architectural style of the time, by the position of the Church in society and by its understanding of the world and of itself. One could almost say that ecclesiology is given an objective form in the buildings of the Church. The Gothic church corresponds to the ecclesiastical claims to dominion enshrined in Pope Gregory VII's *Dictatus papae*. The Baroque buildings of Rome attempt to crystallize and preserve the illusion of a "perfect society". The "historical" style of the nineteenth century looks, like theology, to the Middle Ages. A positive encounter with the modern world is rejected, for the Church forms a world of its own. The Church as "mystical body" is mirrored in the religious buildings of men like R. Schwarz and D. Böhms.

The parallel development of ecclesiastical architecture and ecclesiology is probably most clearly perceptible today because they are both being called radically into question. A simple synthesis of present-day tendencies is impossible in either field. Both seek a right relationship to the world in which they want to proclaim the Christian message of the liberation of man to be himself.

Translated by J. R. Foster

Biographical Notes

ALFONSO ALVAREZ BOLADO, S.J., was born 15 March 1928 in Valladolid and ordained in 1958. He studied at the University of Barcelona, at the Jesuit Faculty of Theology of San Cugat del Vallés (Barcelona) and at the Faculty of Theology of Innsbruck. Master of arts, licentiate of theology and doctor of philosophy, he is director of the Institute "Fe y Secularidad" (University of Madrid) and consultor of the papal Secretariat for Non-Believers. His publications include *Teología de la Muerte de Dios* (1969).

JOSEPH ARNTZ, O.P., was born 20 May 1919 at Nijmegen and ordained in 1943. He studied at the University of Nijmegen. Doctor of theology and of philosophy, he is professor of ethics at the High School of Economics of Tilburg. He has written essays on atomic war, on scientific problems, on the relation between politics and ethics, and on natural law and history, etc.

JOSEPH COMBLIN was born 22 March 1923 in Brussels and ordained in 1947. Doctor of theology, he is professor of theology at the Regional Seminary of the North-East, Recife (Brazil). Among his published works are: *Théologie de la Paix* (Paris, Vol. I 1960, Vol. II 1963) and *Le Christ dans l'Apocalypse* (Paris, 1965).

ANDREW M. GREELEY was born 5 February 1928 in Oak Park (U.S.A.) and ordained in 1954. He studied in the U.S.A. at St Mary of the Lake Seminary and at Chicago University. Master of arts, licentiate of theology, doctor of sociology, he is lecturer on sociology at Chicago University and senior study director of the National Opinion Research Center of the same university. Among his published works are: *The Hesitant Pilgrim: American Catholicism after the Council* (New York, 1966) and *A Future to Hope In* (New York, 1969).

WALTER HOLLENWEGER was born 1 June 1927 in Antwerp, and is a Protestant. He studied at the Universities of Basle and Zurich. Doctor of theology, he is secretary for evangelism at the World Council of Churches in Geneva. Among his publications is *Handbuch der Pfingstbewegung* (9 vols.).

FRANÇOIS HOUTART was born 7 March 1925 in Brussels and ordained in

1949. He studied at Louvain University, at the Institute of Urbanism in Brussels and at Chicago University. Licentiate of social and political sciences, with a diploma in urbanology, he is director of the Centre of Socio-Religious Research at Louvain University. Among his published works are: *Los Cristianos en la Revolucion de America Latina* (in collaboration with E. Pin) (Buenos Aires, 1966) and *Le problème religieux en milieu urbain* (Mons, 1966).

LEO LAEYENDECKER was born in 1930 in Utrecht and is a Catholic. He studied at the University of Amsterdam. Doctor of sociology, he is lecturer in sociology at the same university. Among his publications is *Religie en Conflict* (Meppel, 1967).

JOHANNES BAPTIST METZ was born 5 August 1928 in Welluck (Germany) and ordained in 1954. He studied at the Universities of Innsbruck and Munich. Doctor of philosophy and of theology, he is professor of fundamental theology at the University of Münster. Among his published works are: *Christliche Anthropozentrik* (Munich, 1962) and *Weltverständnis im Glauben* (Mainz, 1965).

KARL RAHNER, S.J., was born 5 March 1904 in Freiburg-im-Breisgau and ordained in 1932. He studied at the Universities of Freiburg and Innsbruck. Doctor of theology, he is professor of dogmatics and of the history of dogma at the University of Münster. Among his published works are: *Schriften zur Theologie* (8 vols, Einsiedeln, 1954–67) and *Sendung und Gnade* (Innsbruck, 1961³). Many of his books have been translated into English and other languages.

MICHAEL RASKE was born 26 May 1936 in Hannover and ordained in 1961. He studied at Freiburg-im-Breisgau, Innsbruck and Paderborn. Doctor of theology, he is assistant at the Catholic Institute of Ecumenism at the University of Münster.

TRUTZ RENDTORFF was born 24 January 1931 in Schwerin (Germany) and is an Evangelical Lutheran. Doctor of theology, he is a professor at the University of Munich. Among his publications are: *Die soziale Struktur der Gemeinde* (1959) and *Kirche und Theologie* (1966).

LUDWIG RÜTTI was born 19 July 1936 in Emmenbrücke (Switzerland) and ordained in 1962. He studied at the Missionary Seminary of Schöneck (Switzerland) and at the University of Münster. Doctor of theology, he is assistant at the Institute of Missiology of the University of Münster.

KLAUS SCHÄFER was born 3 June 1936 at Stuttgart and was ordained in 1968. He studied at the Universities of Tübingen, Bonn, Munich and Copenhagen. Doctor of theology, he is assistant at the Catholic Faculty of Theology at the University of Tübingen.

HEINZ SCHLETTE was born 28 July 1931 in Wesel-Rhein (Germany) and is a Catholic. He studied at the Universities of Münster and Munich. Doctor of theology and of philosophy, he is professor of philosophy at the High School of Pedagogy in Bonn and assistant professor at the University of Sarrebruck. Among his published works are: *Sowjethumanismus* (Kösel, 1960) and *Die Konfrontation mit den Religionen* (Bochum-Cologne, 1964).

International Publishers of CONCILIUM

ENGLISH EDITION
Herder and Herder, Inc.
New York, U.S.A.

Burns & Oates Ltd.
P.O. Box 497
London, S.W.7

DUTCH EDITION
Uitgeverij Paul Brand, N.V.
Hilversum, Netherlands

FRENCH EDITION
Maison Mame
Tours/Paris, France

JAPANESE EDITION (PARTIAL)
Nansôsha
Tokyo, Japan

GERMAN EDITION
Verlagsanstalt Benziger & Co., A.G.
Einsiedeln, Switzerland

Matthias Grunewald-Verlag
Mainz, W. Germany

SPANISH EDITION
Ediciones Cristianidad
Salamanca, Spain

PORTUGUESE EDITION
Livraria Morais Editoria, Ltda.
Lisbon, Portugal

ITALIAN EDITION
Editrice Queriniana
Brescia, Italy

POLISH EDITION (PARTIAL)
Pallottinum
Poznań, Poland